The Strategies of Australia's Universities

Timothy Devinney • Grahame Dowling

The Strategies of Australia's Universities

Revise & Resubmit

palgrave
macmillan

Timothy Devinney
University of Manchester
Alliance Manchester Business School
Manchester, UK

Grahame Dowling
University of Technology
Sydney, Australia

ISBN 978-981-15-3396-9 ISBN 978-981-15-3397-6 (eBook)
https://doi.org/10.1007/978-981-15-3397-6

This Palgrave Macmillan imprint is published by the registered company Springer Nature Singapore Pte Ltd.
The registered company address is: 152 Beach Road, #21-01/04 Gateway East, Singapore 189721, Singapore

Preface

Like many inquiring essays, this one started with some personal intuitions. One is that Australia's public universities are not working as well as they could or should be. Another is that they and many of their overseas counterparts have changed in ways that many older academics dislike and distrust. So to confirm these feelings, we did a quick Google search to see if other people also had misgivings about the university system. The names of the following books suggest that we are not the only people to have reservations about how Australia's universities and others around the world are being managed:

- *Shakespeare, Einstein, and the Bottom Line: The Marketing of Higher Education*
- *Academic Capitalism and the New Economy*
- *University Inc.*
- *The University in Ruins*
- *Our Underachieving Colleges*
- *The Enterprise University: Power, Governance and Re-invention in Australian Higher Education*
- *The Last Professors: The Corporate University and the Fate of the Humanities*
- *Grade Inflation: A Crisis in College Education*
- *Degree Mills: The Billion-Dollar Industry That Has Sold over a Million Fake Diplomas*

- *No University Is an Island*
- *Education! Education! Education! Managerial Ethics and the Law of Unintended Consequences*
- *Digital Diploma Mills: The Automation of Higher Education*
- *From Higher Aims to Hired Hands: The social Transformation of American Business Schools and the Unfulfilled Promise of Management as a Profession*
- *The Knowledge Factory*
- *Creating Entrepreneurial Universities*
- *The Uses of the University*
- *Higher Education in America*
- *Beyond the Ivory Tower*
- *Unmaking the Public University*
- *Markets in Higher Education*
- *Science in the Private Interest*
- *Knowledge & Money*
- *A Manifesto for the Public University*
- *The University in a Corporate Culture*
- *Wannabe U: Inside the Corporate University*
- *The Higher Learning in America*
- *In Pursuit of Prestige*
- *Capitalizing Knowledge*
- *The University, State, and Market*
- *MIT and the Rise of Entrepreneurial Science*
- *The New Production of Knowledge*
- *The Fall of the Faculty: The Rise of the All-Administrative University and Why IT Matters*
- *The Rise of the All-Administrative University and Why It Matters*
- *The Metric Tide*
- *The Commodification of Academic Research: Science and the Modern University*
- *Academic Capitalism and the New Economy: Markets, State and Higher Education*
- *Changing Academic Life* (www.changingacademiclife.com/blog).

There is also vast scholarly literature dealing with the universities and the higher-education sector. Scanning this literature reveals that very little attention has been paid to the strategies of individual universities. This is the focus of this book.

We take a forensic approach to evaluating university strategy. A formal framework is introduced, and like a recent review of UK university strategy by Mike Baxter, public statements of strategy from various universities are used to 'fill in the blanks'.[1] As a reviewer of this title remarked, this approach is both a strength and a weakness of the analysis that follows. Its strength is that it provides a new lens through which to examine university governance and strategy. Its weakness is that the use of a business logic may oversimplify what is essentially a very complex issue. However, looking at universities as though they are quasi-commercial organisations rather than purely educational organisations administered with a public (sector) management (NPM) mindset puts more focus on the economics of a university than will be found in much of the scholarly literature. An economic perspective also highlights some of the uncomfortable issues and trade-offs facing universities around the world.

Our forensic approach is guided by the literature on strategy formulation and implementation in commercial organisations. This is what we taught to MBA students in business schools and what we were invited into companies and professional service firms to discuss. Our approach is also guided by our experience as business school professors in a variety of universities over the last 30 years. Here we saw the transformative effects of new public management on university life.

Manchester, UK — Timothy Devinney
Sydney, NSW, Australia — Grahame Dowling

Note

1. M. Baxter, *University Strategy 2020: Analysis and Benchmarking of the Strategies of UK Universities* (Goal Atlas Ltd., 2019).

Executive Summary

Over the last few decades universities in Australia and overseas have been criticised for not meeting the expectations of the societies in which they operate. Because Australian universities play roles similar to those of their overseas peers, the ideas we present are more broadly applicable to just Australian universities.

One criticism is that universities are not adequately responding to the pressure to make education more affordable and relevant to what has become known as the knowledge economy. Graduates are not 'job ready'. Another criticism is that universities have lost the trust and authority to guide debate on issues such as climate change. The scepticism about climate science amongst many politicians and members of the general public is a good example. We believe that both criticisms are symptomatic of an underlying problem, namely that many universities lack a cogent strategy for what they should be doing and, just as importantly, what they should not be doing.

This book reviews the organisational-level or corporate strategies of some of Australia's prominent universities. It is based on their public documents that boldly proclaim their role in society and how they intend to navigate the future. These statements are written to proclaim relevance, showcase achievements, attract students and help gain the support of government, donors and the communities in which they operate.

Notwithstanding their public relations tone, they are insightful because they provide a window through which one can assess the quality of university strategy and the thinking that developed it. A well-crafted strategy provides confidence in the management of the institution, while a poorly crafted strategy signals that the university is probably wandering into the future.

As the subtitle of the book suggests, we think that most of these strategy statements are deficient. Had they been submitted as a journal article, they would have been desk-rejected; that is, they are so poorly structured that the editors would not send them out for peer review. And for those that were viewed as worthy of peer review, all would be asked for a major revision, a 'revise and resubmit'. This is a harsh evaluation and one that afflicts the strategy statements of many universities around the world and many other organisations. As the book notes, most so-called corporate strategies are incomplete in some key areas and thus are deficient road maps for the future.

The standard against which these strategies are reviewed is that of a basic strategy course taught in a business school. This is a university standard. Hence, if the university cannot pass its own standard, its members and stakeholders should be concerned.

Here is a snapshot of the major problems revealed by our analysis of the published organisational-level strategies of Australia's universities.

Strategy Statements

- Most strategy statements lack a coherent story about how the actions of the university are contributing to its evolutionary fitness. Rather, they are couched as public relations communications that lack any anxiety that should accompany the current circumstances. This undermines their credibility as a blueprint for guiding and running the organisation. It also invites many members of the university to regard them as public relations blather.
- The template from which the strategy is crafted is not evident. What results is a document containing many fragments of strategy but no overall coherent strategy.

- In the hope of signalling their social credentials, many universities emphasise hygiene factors and diversity policies in their strategy statements. This often provides a confusing picture of the institution's main purpose.
- Many crucial areas of strategy are missing such as the nature of competition and/or collaboration amongst universities; the competitive advantage or disadvantage of the institution; operational and dynamic capabilities; the risk profile of the institution; the role of budgets; how the design of the organisation helps or hinders its aims; the alignment between individual, faculty and institutional measures of performance; the optimal staffing profile of the institution; the optimal size of the institution and the fundamental business model of the university.

Strategic Issues

- The councils or equivalent oversight bodies of Australia's universities are staffed more with volunteer laypersons than with professional directors. Many members do not have the capabilities to check and challenge their vice chancellor's strategic initiatives.
- Most universities have essentially the same set of grand aims, structures and product offerings which contributes to a lack of educational diversity across the higher-education system. They have distinction without significant difference.
- In most universities a large and complex managerial bureaucracy surrounds the operations of the faculties. This organisational complexity filters down to create individual complexity for many employees. It also marginalises the contribution of its academic staff.
- There is often no direct line-of-sight between the grand aims of the university and many of the key performance indicators of academic staff. Thus, there is a distinct tendency to 'hope for A but reward B'.
- Most universities promote a fragmented social justice mission that is more bolted onto rather than built into their primary functions of education and research.[1]

- University rankings (which reflect a competitive mindset) are being substituted for harder-to-measure, but more meaningful, goals (such as intellectual and educational quality).
- The universities are too costly to run. Each requires the expenditure of hundreds of millions of dollars annually before a single class is taught or a research paper written.
- The universities are struggling to capitalise (capture value from) part of one of their largest costs and what is a distinct competitive advantage, namely, their research.
- Many universities are severing the nexus between teaching and research. This degrades the competitive advantage they have over other organisations that provide education or research.
- Most universities do not have sufficient endowments to provide independence from changes in government funding.
- While there is much discussion that the current educational model is outdated, there is little consensus on what should be a viable alternative.
- The universities are reluctant to discuss, let alone confront, the tension between meeting financial targets and upholding academic standards.

This list of issues does not predict the demise of Australia's universities. Unlike some media commentary about how these institutions need fundamental reinvention, our analysis suggests that to significantly enhance their evolutionary fitness, they need some significant renovations. We do not specify any particular strategy as best for one or more of Australia's universities. However, we will argue that the multiversity or comprehensive or diversified conglomerate nature of Australia's public universities (it goes by many names) could easily be simplified. Or if it is to be retained, this organisational design needs far less bureaucratic oversight than it currently receives.

Our plea to the mandarins that run and oversee Australia's public universities is that they create more comprehensive and coherent strategies for what they want to do, because at present many of these institutions look more like an organised anarchy than a well-designed, well-run public institution.[2]

Notes

1. By 'bolted-on' we mean that there is no direct relationship between a social justice activity and the two core activities of the university. Many social justice initiatives are added into a university by policy fiat.
2. The term *organised anarchy* was coined in 1974 by M. D. Cohen and J. G. March, *Leadership and Ambiguity: The American College President* (New York: McGraw-Hill, 1974), to describe universities. It seems that so little has changed.

Contents

List of Figures

1

Australia's Universities

As a species, universities are one of the oldest recognisable forms of organisation in the Western Hemisphere. Their foundation principles were established by the ancient Greeks. Since then they have withstood wars, revolutions, political purges, economic depressions, technology innovations and industrial transformations. In Australia they have also withstood numerous government enquiries and policy shifts.[1] The survival and importance of universities speak to the immutability of their purpose and their ability to adapt.

In their book *The Enterprise University* Simon Marginson and Mark Considine use history and location to segment Australia's public universities into five groups:[2]

- Sandstone universities, named as such because of some of their prominent buildings. The Universities of Adelaide, Melbourne and Sydney are good examples. These were also the foundation universities in each state.
- Redbrick universities, founded after World War II. They include the Australian National University, the University of New South Wales

T. Devinney, G. Dowling, *The Strategies of Australia's Universities*,
https://doi.org/10.1007/978-981-15-3397-6_1

and Monash University. These universities had some prominent (and ugly) red brick buildings.

- Gumtree universities, founded between 1960 and 1975, like the University of Newcastle and Griffith University, many of which are set in (gumtree) bushland settings.
- Unitechs which are the largest of the old colleges of advanced education like Queensland University of Technology and the University of Technology Sydney.
- New universities which are a mixed group of post-1986 universities like Southern Cross University and Edith Cowan University.

Marginson and Considine note that once a university becomes part of a group, it is hard for it to leave. These institutional identities are sticky. They also note that the older Sandstone universities have developed an identity as the establishment universities that they protect as a special place in the higher-education system.[3] However, while the universities look different from the outside, they argue that these institutions are all quite similar in their size (mid-size), course offerings (many and varied), values (excellence) and aspirations (growth).

1.1 The Grand Bargain

Australian public universities are largely funded by the state and have been allowed to be self-governed. The state has entered into a Grand Bargain with its universities as described in part by the Australian Government Productivity Commission:

> A well-functioning higher education system should provide students with opportunities and empower them to make the choice of whether or not to study. It should match students with suitable study opportunities and meet the needs of the labour market. It should be open to people regardless of their background. It should also encourage those who will benefit most from the many years spent acquiring a qualification, and support students to succeed while at university, recognising that university education is costly to students and the public more generally. Productivity Commission,

The Demand Driven University System: A Mixed Report Card, Commission Research Paper, Canberra, 2019, p. 2

This is the demand requirement of the bargain. On the supply side the federal and state governments provide base funding for the universities. For top-up funding these governments sanction creating commercial relationships with industry and the capitalisation of university research. They also provide favourable conditions for attracting domestic and international fee-paying students.

The Grand Bargain comes with many rules and regulations. Each university is governed by its establishment legislation. The government also polices its public universities through various oversight and quality assurance bodies. And the federal government of the day via the Minister for Education plays a key role in shaping policy. This institutional structure requires constant attention and often creates frustration for university administrators. It also imposes significant governance and financial costs on each university.

The Grand Bargain grants universities a privileged position to provide higher education and a gatekeeping role to award degrees and help accredit a broad range of workforce occupations. The benefit to universities in this two-sided market, matching students with the perceived needs of the workplace, is to concentrate power in the hands of a small number of institutions. The benefit to graduates is that they receive credible credentials, which, in turn, provide more opportunities in life and work. In general, graduates do financially better than people without a university education. The benefit to the state is that it receives a good (tax) return from its investment in graduate education.

The Grand Bargain also resonates with a fundamental premise of contemporary higher education, namely that 'knowledge is now the universal currency that underpins the relative performance and success of individuals, organizations and nations' (Professor Paul Johnson, the vice chancellor of the University of Western Australia).[4] Professor Johnson is talking about the knowledge economy. Because many universities around the world have bought into this idea, it is worthwhile describing what the Organization for Economic Cooperation and Development suggests it means:[5]

> The knowledge economy is an expression coined to describe trends in advanced economies towards greater dependence on knowledge, information and high skill levels, and the increasing need for ready access to all of these by business and public sectors.

Luckily for the universities, a growing knowledge economy provides an economic tailwind for the university sector because it demands more graduates and more research. However, as noted in the next section, looking at education and research as economic products provides a distorted lens through which to manage universities and calibrate their outcomes.

As noted earlier, a part of the Grand Bargain is that university education will be available to all suitable students who wish to acquire it. However, this idea of a university education for the 'masses' has been challenged as a waste of public money, especially if it is designed to produce 'job-ready' graduates. As Bran Caplan notes, because much of the current university education is the study of irrelevancies, it results in empty credentials.[6] As many graduates in arts, psychology, law, politics, science and media studies will testify, much of what they learn in their degree is of little relevance to the job they do or the life they lead. In many industries you learn more on the job than any university education can provide.

So the role of many degrees is to signal that you can apply yourself successfully to a big task, rather than you have gained a body of relevant knowledge and been assessed against a standard of proficiency. Here a degree helps get a job interview. For example, some of the large professional accounting firms who recruit large numbers of graduates are becoming degree-agnostic.[7] Outstanding performance in any degree is what they are looking for.

Notwithstanding the concerns about the instrumental value of much higher education, currently we are seeing the universities doubling up in this labour certification game. First, as more and more people gain an undergraduate degree, the demand for postgraduate degrees rises to signal that the holder is better than his or her peers. Next we see universities talking about the benefits of their 'lifelong learning' programmes. The key issue here is that the personal, social and economic benefits of university-based life-long learning are yet to be clearly shown. For example, in the corporate world there are a number of so-called academy companies like General Electric and BP, and consulting firms like McKinsey & Company that offer far better post-university management training than any Australian university. BP's Financial University offers more than 300 courses for the company's top 250 financial managers.[8] General Electric's Financial Management Programme runs for two years and involves assignments in various company roles. Because of the quality of these programmes, many graduates are poached by other companies. No Australian university can match the breadth and depth of these types of career-based lifelong learning programmes. So if universities are educating for the knowledge economy, they might want to reconsider where their comparative advantage lies.

Another part of the Grand Bargain with public universities is that they will be efficient, transparent and accountable. Since the 1980s the new public management movement has sought to achieve these outcomes. Because it explains why Australia's public universities and many of its counterparts around the world are governed the way they are, we review its underlying logic.

1.2 New Public Management

Thomas Diefenbach notes that new public management (NPM) is a set of beliefs and value statements about how public sector organisations should be designed, organised and managed, and how in a quasi-business manner they should function.[9] The basic idea is to make these organisations more business-like (the assumption here is better managed) and market-oriented (the assumption here is offering greater value-for-money). The benchmark against which progress is judged is that of the 'old' public sector organisations that were over-formalised, slow, compartmentalised, inefficient and red-tape-producing bureaucracies. In the university context, these institutions were often infected with so-called stagnant consensus seeking, whereby any organised group could slow or veto a decision. Much so-called collegiate debate was boring and time-wasting. And many parts of the university were ruled by 'god professors' and privilege.

Diefenbach notes that these NPM ideas are now applied to all types of public sector organisations in most Western nations and they are supported by all the major political parties. There is much written about NPM by academics,[10] and nearly all of it is uncomplimentary as it applies to universities.[11] Professional university managers would undoubtedly see things differently. Notwithstanding these opposing views, the ideas and practices of NPM are now entrenched in many universities around the world.

In the university context an underlying belief is that because higher education is largely funded by taxpayers, they and their political masters are entitled to know that their money is well spent. Thus, efficiency is a key metric of performance. Therefore, guided by their managers, universities now measure and create benchmarks for activities like the time and cost of educating different types of students, and the inputs (such as research grants) and outputs (such as journal articles) of research. Given that academics are the significant cost component in these activities, it is not surprising that the search for cost efficiency has resulted in a worsening of the faculty/student ratio, a decrease in the number of tenured faculty and an increase in the number of itinerant 'adjunct' teachers. For education, process efficiency is being sought by asking students to do more education by themselves 'on-line'.

Another focus of NPM is quality or excellence—of research and education. But these are slippery concepts. What is easy to measure is outputs adjusted for quality. Favourite metrics for research are the number of articles published in international 'top-tier' peer-reviewed journals and the number of citations they receive. Another is the amount of research money raised. An emerging metric is the 'impact' or outcome of this research, now formalised in Australia as the Engagement and Impact (EI) Assessment. Favourite metrics for education are the completion rate of students, satisfaction with the course and the instructor, and the percentage of students who are employed soon after graduation.

Another focus of NPM is transparency and accountability. Inputs and outputs need to be identified, measured, audited and reported. A look at a university's annual operational and financial reports will swamp the casual reader with such data. They might also be surprised by the number of operational and compliance issues that a university must address.

Another aspect of transparency, accountability and quality is the increasing scrutiny by outside quality assurance agencies. Some like Excellence in Research Australia (ERA) are government sanctioned, but many like the so-called reputation rankings are private. What these agencies measure inevitably filters through to what the universities think is important and strategic.

The two issues of quality and transparency have led to some absurd reductionist outcomes sanctioned by university administration. One is the setting of academic benchmarks for managing research performance. For example, at one of our universities a recent scheme started with the goal to be a Top 3 Australian Business School as recognised by the ERA. It then defined research quality as the publication of articles in A* and A journals as designated by the journal list used in the ERA evaluations. Each journal was awarded points (*A** = 2.5 points and *A* = 1 point). While the research benchmarks said that other things matter (such as PhD supervision and securing external research money), its emphasis was that these publications <u>really</u> matter. When publications appeared outside these journals, they were recalibrated as journal points (e.g., a book with a prestigious academic publisher was 2.5 points).[12] So here we find that an individual's research performance is essentially reduced to a specified minimum number of 'publication points'. Some commentators have characterised such schemes as resembling the old Soviet planning goals. They also make a mockery of university narrative statements noted in Chap. 2 that talk about how our universities are tackling the complex, multidisciplinary problems facing society.

Another key belief of NPM in universities is that education and research are, or can be, characterised as economic goods. This also sits comfortably with the belief of an emerging information economy. When research is an economic good it needs to pay for itself. So we see the search for more external funding and opportunities to 'sell' its intellectual property. This partly explains why universities are interested in measuring research impact. Impactful research, and the academics who do such work, are easier to 'sell' to funding agencies, industry, politicians and the media.

Education as an economic good defines its key attribute as a qualification, and its benefit as a return-on-investment, usually employment.

Also, it implies that the process of education is an economic transaction between a buyer (students) and seller (the university, faculty and teachers that delivered the education). Thus, it is not surprising that students approach this transaction like the consumers they are in other domains. They want value for money (such as a qualification that helps to get a job) and satisfaction (they liked the education process). This is especially so if they are affluent consumers, namely, high-fee-paying (international) students. In this consumer context, the hierarchical relationship between teacher and student can easily disappear. And when university managers decide that more horizontal (peer-to-peer) and self-learning approaches to education are desirable, it does. Finally, with the need for growth in student numbers to finance operations, many universities have degraded the signal quality of the value of their qualifications. Grade inflation,[13] falling entry standards[14] and contract student cheating[15] are three prominent causes.

There are two paradoxes and two design faults in NPM that bedevil universities. The first paradox is that as the universities strive for greater efficiency and effectiveness, they require greater numbers of managers to design, oversee and report on the systems implemented. Our contention is that too many of these managers add friction to the institution's operational efficiency because they then require compliance work from the front-line academics. The criticism here is that managers often regard the time of academics as a free good that can be conscripted for all manner of meetings, procedure following activities and report writing. For example, at the time of writing, to make sure that all examinations look similar, the University of Technology Sydney requires both the examiner and another assessor to review 29 criteria for four different versions of each exam (the main, rescheduled, alternative and supplementary exams). There are 145 boxes (yes, the form has little boxes) to be ticked by two people and an associate dean who checks that the form is complete! This is a wonderful example of box-ticking compliance. It is also costly in terms of time and tedium.

The second paradox is that as Australia's public universities mirror the corporate form, there is a renewed internal emphasis that they should not forget to act like old-fashioned public service organisations. The tactic here is for the institutions to adopt and promote the ethos of impartiality, social equity, fairness, integrity, citizenship, representation, welfare and social justice. There is nothing wrong with these ideals except that they often deflect attention away from what a university is really about. It is not a public sector organisation. It is a 'university', an organisation that we call throughout this book as an intellectual capital organisation. The primary reputation of these organisations is based on the development and dissemination of ideas and information, not its hygiene, namely, being efficient and equitable places in which to work and study.

The first design fault is that NPM characterises a university as a machine that can be managed with numerical targets and performance measures. Because it has multiple constituencies, a framework like Robert Kaplan and David Norton's balanced scorecard is ideal for this purpose.[16] However, for anybody who has actually worked in the blast furnace of a university, a better characterisation is that these institutions are systems of human relationships. These are especially powerful in the research context where people work together to generate new knowledge. (For example, today there are few single-authored publications.) The NPM obsession of looking good by the numbers does violence to one's understanding of the sense of community in a university.

The second design fault with NPM is that it overemphasises efficiency and its companions, accountability and transparency. Many years before NPM became the vogue, the founding father of modern management, Peter Drucker, observed that focusing on efficiency often results in an inability to find opportunity:

> The pertinent question is not how to do things right, but how to find the right things to do.[17]

So NPM ideas put blinkers on universities who are now required by their principal funding agencies to seek more opportunities.

NPM explains how and why the central administration of many universities has grown and extracted control from the faculties. It also suggests one reason why many universities seem to be worried about their future, namely, that they are not good in identifying and exploiting opportunities. Because NPM is the grounding managerial belief system in university administration, we will use a complementary business-oriented framework (Chap. 3) as a lens to evaluate it and the strategies of Australia's public universities.

1.3 The Current Report Card

Australia's universities are important to the economy and its social fabric. Some of the raw numbers are impressive, such as they inject over $30 billion into the economy each year; they account for in excess of 1.5% of GDP; international students are the third-largest (reverse) export, accounting for more than $20 billion annually; and from approximately 0.3% of the world's population, Australian universities produce approximately 3% of its scientific research.

At the sector level these universities provide a great return on investment. For example, in a speech to the National Press Club (14 August 2018), Professor Ian Jacobs (President and Vice Chancellor of UNSW and Chair of the Group-of-Eight Universities) outlined that these universities provide a tenfold return on the government's investment (as calculated by the group London Economics).[18] He also went on to argue that this economic return could be even greater if there was better business-university collaboration. In a report titled *The Importance of Universities to Australia's Prosperity* the consulting firm Deloitte Access Economics catalogued how Australia's universities also make a range of significant contributions to Australia's social fabric.[19]

From a management perspective we see a problem with Australia's universities. They are too complex. Much of this complexity is caused by government regulations, policies, funding formulas and reporting requirements. Government ministers keep changing the settings of these levers of control. However, a significant amount of complexity is self-inflicted. As the universities try to accommodate an ever-broadening array of concerns, they add programmes, policies and procedures without the discipline of removing or consolidating some existing provisions. Institutional complexity inevitably seeps down to congest the delivery of front-line services. Here we focus on self-inflicted complexity and the reasons why it persists.

From a risk perspective we see two weak spots for most of Australia's universities. These are at the very top and bottom of the institutions. At the top is the governance regime. This is 'designed to fail'. It is discussed in Chap. 2. At the bottom is the trend that an increasing number of undergraduate students seem to be adopting the attitude of 'consumer' rather than 'student'. Thus their relationship with and loyalty to a particular university is weak. This issue is discussed in Chap. 5. In contrast, a strength of Australia's universities is that the Tertiary Education Quality and Standards Agency suggests that they have low financial risk. However, the fallout from COVID-19 pandemic illustrated that this evaluation was somewhat optimistic.

One of Australia's more noteworthy vice chancellors Professor Glyn Davis notes that in 2015–16 the American sociologist William Lacy found much to like about our public universities—for their size and resources, they performed well in research and education, contributed to the community and were admired internationally.[20] However, the qualification to his positive report card was that they lacked diversity and thus offered few meaningful choices to students about the type of institution to attend. We also suggest that they are an expensive way to deliver higher education. And to offset these costs, the reliance on overseas students as a significant revenue stream has led some universities to degrade their entry standards to the point that these marginal students struggle to cope with university life, and thus the reputation of the institution suffers.[21]

From a strategic perspective some other profile numbers that have been variously reported about Australia's universities are thought-provoking. For example, it costs $12.4 billion annually to operate the Group of Eight universities, of which the government provided $6.7 billion; more than half the number of people who work in our universities are not academics; in seven years our universities spent $1.7 billion in marketing and advertising; at the time of writing the highest-paid vice chancellor gets a salary of $1.53 million.[22] In comparison, the prime minister of Australia and the president of the United States earn less than many of our vice chancellors. These numbers hint at a central question explored in this title, namely, are our universities bloated with administrative costs? Our thesis is that Australia's universities are burdened by their managerial bureaucracies.

1.4 Are Australia's Universities Top-Heavy?

We just claimed that Australia's universities have fewer academic staff than administrative staff. For example, the 2018 University of Technology's Annual Report of Operations noted that it had 1881 academic staff and 2102 professional staff (page 1). This is a professional to academic or 'administrative intensity' ratio of 1.12. Trawling the websites of Australia's other public universities reveals that most have ratios of 1.0 or greater. Intuitively (at least to us) this seems high.

To support our intuition, we note a study of 115 UK universities by Rhys Andrews and his colleagues.[23] Their data found that these universities had a ratio of 0.46 (with a range of 0.34–0.66). Thus, Australia's universities have twice the administrative overhead as their UK counterparts. So which ratio might be the better one?

As Andrews and his colleagues note, the literature on administrative intensity in public sector organisations suggests that there is an inverted U-shaped relationship between administrative intensity and performance whereby as administrative intensity rises, this work may expand beyond its usefulness for supporting the core activities of the organisation. Their empirical study set out to explore this issue. Three of their findings are insightful (and support our academic intuition):

- There was support for the inverted U-shaped relation for both research and education performance, and the tipping point was a ratio of approximately 0.50.
- Administrative intensity is helpful up to 0.50 in dealing with external regulatory forces (such as the ERA) and external market pressures (such as winning research grants, recruiting students and placing them in employment). After this point it starts to create administrative friction.
- Students are happier with their education when resources are allocated to the front-line rather than back-office functions.

If we accept the essence of these findings, the strategic challenge for many universities is to reduce the number of administrators. But where should cuts occur? The findings suggest that administrative effects are positive when they directly support front-line education and research. Many of these staff can be found in the faculties, laboratories and research centres. The findings also suggest that administrative effects are positive when they provide education and research resources for the faculties, such as recruiting students and helping to secure research funding. Their work supports an old management consulting mantra in the service industry that says that the administrators who matter most are the people who serve the front-line people. Before academics started to use Microsoft Office to design and produce much of their teaching and research, these second-row people were an army of secretaries and research assistants. Today many academics do many of the jobs previously done by these people. In our working careers, Microsoft Office is probably the single most useful and effective cost-saving business process innovation adopted throughout universities.

So where do administrative inefficiencies lie? Our contention as (old) front-line service providers is that one source emanates from the compliance regime that universities have created to manage to government regulations and the expectations of being a public sector organisation. For example, everybody is required to complete, and periodically renew their certification for an increasing number of training modules concerning the design of their education materials, and their workplace knowledge and behaviour.

A second source inefficiency is the desire of university administrators to dictate how education should be conducted. For example, university-wide teaching systems, many of which have yet to demonstrate their efficacy, are imposed on courses that may not be suited to their approach. And they often don't suit the teaching style of the instructor. So what often results is a box-ticking compliance response. For example, in many cases course syllabi read like legal documents, with more than half their content made up of administrative details that have no relevance to the course being taught and are simply included to meet compliance requirements. Few students read this material, and many instructors don't know what it really means. But ultimately, teaching material is adjusted to comply with the current standard. Then after some grumbling by the instructors, life goes on as before.

A third source of inefficiency is the back-office systems of universities, such as human resources and information technology. As the commercial providers of the software that powers these systems evolve and upgrades are installed (to the software company's profit), hundreds of staff struggle to reconfigure their systems to accommodate changes which are often superfluous. What system-wide information technology change forgets is that there are three types of staff (and students) in a university: those who interpret IT to mean inspiration technology, those for whom it means information technology and those for whom these two letters mean in trouble.

To illustrate the amounts of money that might be saved by making even modest reductions in administrative intensity, consider that in 2018 the University of Technology Sydney spent $296.5 million on non-academic salaries and $12.4 million on software maintenance (2018 Financial Report, p. 22). A 10% saving here would have increased the university's operating surplus by over 40%.

1.5 Why This Book

This book starts at a point of agreement with one of Australia's more notable vice chancellors, Glyn Davis of the University of Melbourne. As he moved on from this position, he made the salutary point that strategy really matters.

> One responsibility matters for everyone within the university: strategy. Guiding the priorities that mean we do some things but not others, that we ensure the university articulates, and lives by, its aspirations.
>
> Strategy requires a full armoury of skills—values, vision, clarity, communication, an implementation plan, evaluation, reporting back. It means sharing with colleagues a sense of purpose, why this place matters.
>
> G. Davis, "Confessions of a Vice Chancellor", *The Australian Financial Review* (30 August, 2018), 52–3.

The reason for this book is that we believe that our universities have lost focus on their two primary roles. All have been distracted by the chatter of politicians, special interest groups and media commentators. They have also struggled to manage the expectations of their primary government paymaster who wants them to do more with less. The essence of our criticism of Australia's public universities is that we can't see that many of these institutions have a comprehensive and coherent strategy. Their public documents are best described as a collection of strategy fragments. Also, the institutions typically look to be too complex and too costly to run. They try to achieve too much with their limited resources which results in many things being less effectively done than they should be. Also, in order to get public support, they make contestable claims that they are underfunded.[24] Our argument is that this is likely to be camouflage for the fact that they squander some of the funding they receive.

In his book *The Australian Idea of a University*, Professor Glyn Davis describes why our universities look the way they are.[25] They are a product of their past—their British heritage, establishment legislation, sources of funding, perceived social obligations, various government interventions and follow-the-leader academic and management mentalities. He suggests that they lack distinctiveness and are ripe for disruption. We agree that imprinting by history, combined with imitative behaviour (isomorphism) caused by the demands of external ratings agencies, following each other's academic norms and voluntary follow-the-leader actions, has led to a lack of distinctiveness. Also, the last two types of imitation are classic institutional risk aversion strategies.

However, there is debate about what type of distinctiveness a university should strive for. Should it reflect the demands of different types and abilities of students? Should it reflect the supply of different courses and teaching styles? Should it reflect the culture of the institution? Or should it reflect cost and educational difficulty that create a status hierarchy of institutions? The last type of distinctiveness allows a university to sort students into layers, which might be something that certain types of employers in the knowledge economy value. Thus, two strategic questions are (a) which type or combination of types of distinctiveness could enhance the evolutionary fitness of the university, and (b) would it be valuable to dilute the various types of isomorphism that bind the institutions together?

While there have been calls for universities to 'disruptively innovate' and provide a new model of university education, we believe that in the short term the current orthodoxy is so strong that it will only result in incremental changes to some universities rather than a radical innovation by any of the incumbents.[26] For a sector with such a long and distinguished history this is not a fatal diagnosis. In a world where many people are being spooked by the rhetoric of turbulent change, to have some long-standing public institutions 'make haste slowly' is a somewhat comforting prospect. The challenge for the university sector is to persuasively communicate the logic of this evolutionary path.

Threats to this make haste slowly scenario come from three sources. One is international in nature. Because our universities play in an international market, a real danger comes from whether countries like India and China decide to mimic the current world-wide university system or break the mould of what higher education really entails. So far the surface indicators are that they seem to be playing the current game. For example, many Chinese universities are 'buying back' from overseas universities their best expatriate academics with huge salaries. Also, as *The Economist* newspaper recently noted, some Chinese universities are being very successful in the orthodox university rankings game, especially on the research front.[27]

The second threat is reconstructionist in nature. W. Chan Kim and Renée Mauborgne of the INSEAD business school have called this strategic mindset the search for blue oceans.[28] Here a new entrant will target the most profitable sectors of the higher education market with a business model and value proposition to students and academics that attract the best of both groups. Part of this will involve developing a research model that is self-funding. This type of institution will have a small, rather than a broad, footprint. A version of it is outlined in Chap. 12.

The third threat is political in nature. It is the increasing tendency for governments to ask universities to rely on market mechanisms to raise new revenue. Because teaching is what raises most revenue, there is a push to grow student numbers. As these numbers grow, many students now come to university without all the basic skills necessary to complete their education. One common missing skill for overseas students is English proficiency. Some students will attend catch-up courses offered by the university to upgrade their language skills; however, many others will muddle through, sometimes with the help of their fellow students. The problem here is that poor language skills impede learning and degrade student interaction in classrooms and tutorials. It also feeds the trend for more examinations to adopt a multiple-choice format. There is also the push to get more research to pay for itself. Thus, research with no immediate commercial benefit may be put at risk.

Two outcomes of these trends are that universities have become better marketers of their education and tougher negotiators about the intellectual property rights of their research with industry. The consequences of these outcomes sometimes surprise universities. For example, students become more like consumers and demand value for money. The teacher-student relationship is redefined. And in the USA, because some universities are tough negotiators of intellectual property, many US companies want to work with overseas universities where they get more favourable intellectual property terms.[29]

1.6 The Roadmap Ahead

To preface our strategic analysis, we start by discussing the nature of the public strategy statements we rely on. These statements can be found on the Internet via searching terms like 'University X strategic plan'. Each one is a narrative about the university's vision and ambitions. While these statements provide only a partial picture of a university's strategy, they are the single best source of information available in the public domain. Also, their publication on university websites indicates that these institutions are proud to use such statements as a motivational device for staff—a good housekeeping seal of approval for government—and to promote the vision and capabilities of the institution.

Next we look at the governance of our universities. This is where the strategy of the university gets 'signed off'. Then we describe what strategy is and is not. This template serves as the road map for our forensic analysis. The various published statements of university strategy provide the feedstock for this analysis. They provide specific examples of good and poor practice to illustrate the points made. We supplement these cases with observations from other commentators and our experience. To conclude our critique, we describe what a new type of Australian university might look like.

Our position is that with more thoughtful strategies, better management and more structural diversity our universities could and should be much better.[30] As two old professors with more than 70 years' combined experience, much of it in the trenches of three Australian universities, and as anybody who has worked in or been a student at an Australian university knows, these institutions are like a curate's egg—they are composed of some good bits and some bad bits.

Our perspective is contrarian. So the aim of the book is to expose some of the bad bits of university strategy so that when fixed, they can support rather than erode the good bits of the curate's egg. Our book follows on from the work of Simon Marginson and Mark Considine in *The Enterprise University: Power, Governance and Re-invention in Australian Higher Education*. This scholarship provides the history of many of the issues we discuss.

Notes

1. For a review of many of these, see S. J. Duckett, "Turning right at the crossroads: The Nelson Reports' proposals to transform Australia's universities', *Higher Education*, Vol. 47 (2004), 211–240.
2. S. Marginson and M. Considine, *The Enterprise University: Power, Governance and Re-invention in Australian Higher Education* (Cambridge, UK: Cambridge University Press, 2000).
3. Establishment here means both the first (establishing) group of universities and that they cater to the establishment/elite sector of the class system.
4. As noted in the university's 2020 vision statement.
5. As noted by the Organization for Economic Cooperation and Development (OECD).
6. B. Caplan, *The Case Against Education* (Princeton: Princeton University Press, 2018).
7. P. Nikoletatos, "Shaping sticky students: encouraging lifelong academic relationships in an era of transience", *Campus Review* (14 June, 2019).

8. Reported in J. Karaian, *The Chief Financial Officer* (New York: Public Affairs, 2014), pp. 56–57.
9. T. Diefenbach, "New Public Management in Public Sector Organizations: The Dark Side of Managerialistic Enlightenment", *Public Administration*, Vol. 87, No. 4 (2009), 892–909.
10. See for example the journals *Public Administration* and *Public Management Review*.
11. See also, C. Lorenz, "If You're So Smart, Why Are You under Surveillance? Universities, Neoliberalism and New Public Management", *Critical Inquiry*, Vol. 38 (2012), 599–629.
12. Notwithstanding the tendency for universities to say in their strategy narratives that staff should be innovative and that they will be respected as individuals, managers like benchmarks that drive conformity because they (a) help to start often difficult conversations with an academic—your position is expected to perform at this level, (b) they define the agenda for the conversation—these are the criteria that the committee agreed on and (c) they appear to be fair in their consideration of a person's case—everybody is judged by the same criteria.
13. See, for example, V. E. Johnson, *Grade Inflation: A Crisis in College Education* (New York: Springer, 2003).
14. See, for example, J. Baker, "Top Uni's Plan to Cut Entry Standards" *The Sydney Morning Herald* (15 June, 2019), 1 & 2.
15. See, for example, the MyMaster scandal.
16. R. S. Kaplan and D. S. Norton, *The Balanced Scorecard: Translating Strategy into Action* (Boston: Harvard Business School Press, 1996). For the counter-human relations view to this approach, see H. T. Johnson and A. Bröms, *Profit Beyond Measure: Extraordinary Results Through Attention to Work and People* (New York: The Free Press, 2000).
17. P. F. Drucker, *Managing for Results* (New York: Harper & Row, 1964), p. 5.
18. Reported in *The Conversation* (14 August, 2018).
19. *The Importance of Universities to Australia's Prosperity* (Barton, ACT: Deloitte Access Economics, 2015).
20. G. Davis, "Confessions of a Vice Chancellor", *The Australian Financial Review* (30 August, 2018), 52–3.
21. See, for example, E. Worthington, S. O'Neill and N. Selvaratnam, "Universities Ignoring Own English Standards to Admit More High-paying International Students", Australian Broadcasting Commission,

Four Corners, screened 6 May, 2019); transcript available at ABC News (abc.et.au).

22. Reported in P. Singhal, "University vice-chancellor salaries soaring past $1.5 million—and set to keep going", *The Sydney Morning Herald* (21 June, 2019). At the time of writing the salary of the Australian Prime Minister was $538,460 and that of the US President was US$450,000.
23. R. Andrews, G. Boyne, and A. M. S. Mostafa, "When Bureaucracy Matters for Organizational Performance: Exploring the Benefits of Administrative Intensity in Big and Complex Organizations", *Public Administration*, Vol. 95, No. 1 (2017), 115–139; Table 1.
24. Given that any increase in government funding for higher education must be at the expense of some other areas of public expenditure or an increase in public debt, it is incumbent on this sector to prove its worth to society before boldly claiming to be underfunded.
25. G. Davis, *The Australian Idea of a University* (Carlton, Vic: Melbourne University Press, 2017).
26. See, for example, H. J. Eyring and C. M. Christensen, *The Innovative University: Changing the DNA of Higher Education from the Inside Out* (San Francisco: Jossey-Bass, 2011).
27. "Looking to beat the world", *The Economist* (17 November, 2018), 33–34.
28. W. Chan Kim and R. Mauborgne, *Blue Ocean Strategy* (Boston: Harvard Business Press, 2005).
29. W. C. Johnson, "Globalisation of Research and Development in a Federated World", in L. E. Weber and J. J. Duderstadt (Eds.), *Reinventing the Research University* (Econmica, 2004), 159–175.
30. For a picture of the diversity of US institutions see R. Zemsky, "On Classifying Universities: Policy, Function and Market", in L. E. Weber and J. J. Duderstadt (Eds.), *Reinventing the Research University* (Econmica, 2004), 109–117.

2

The University Strategy Narrative: Advertisement, Story or Blueprint?

David Barry and Michael Elmes suggest that strategies start with an inherent problem, namely, they are a form of fiction, something that is created and made up.[1] Hence, they pose the same basic challenge faced by other writers of fiction—how to develop an engaging, compelling account that other people will buy into, and in this case implement, or at least implicitly support. So here we look at how universities tell their strategy story. As the subtitle of this chapter suggests, some look like advertisements, some like stories and some like a blueprint for the future. Thus, the vice chancellor is the chief salesperson, storyteller or architect. The strategic questions here are (a) which form is best, and (b) which form is likely to suggest that the university is well managed?

From a diagnostic perspective, what the universities write about themselves under the banner *University Strategy* is the primary source of evidence for the comments we make throughout this book. As we will illustrate throughout this title, we suggest that these are confident but often not competent documents. Our other major source of evidence is the annual operational and financial reports of the universities. In theory, there should be a direct line-of-sight between a university's statement of strategy and these two statements. In practice, this is seldom the case.

T. Devinney, G. Dowling, *The Strategies of Australia's Universities*,
https://doi.org/10.1007/978-981-15-3397-6_2

Few annual reports start with a cogent summary of strategy and then report against this framework. For example, the 2018 University of Technology Sydney Annual Report describes its strategy in 5 bullet points on page 2 of this 55-page report.

2.1 Strategy as Advertisement, Story and Blueprint

The length of a strategy statement and its presentation at the vice chancellor's talking tour that accompanies the launch of a new strategy will indicate its primary role. A cinematic, highly scripted strategy launch generally suggests an advertising or story role. A PowerPoint show with lots of data and frameworks suggests a blueprint. In a subtle way, the type of presentation becomes an attribute of the credibility of the strategy.

A good example of an advertising style of strategy statement was the University of Technology Sydney's statement 'Our Objectives 2009–2018'. It was only two pages long—and presented a bit like an A4-size jigsaw puzzle. (In 2019 it was superseded by a longer story-style statement.) In contrast, the University of Melbourne's statement 'Strategic Plan 2015–2020' was 30 pages long—a story, and the University of New South Wales' plan was 70 pages long—a story and blueprint. Longer statements tend to be more concrete and have more gravitas than shorter statements. Some statements are accompanied by a web-based presentation designed to offer a more customised and interactive experience for the viewer.

Many of the advertising-style strategy statements highlight some (hopefully) memorable slogans, aspects of which appear on mouse mats, coffee cups and university advertising material. And like many corporate advertisements they are targeted primarily at staff and the students who attend open days. They are quickly forgotten. We suggest they trivialise strategy by making it seem more like a marketing programme than a critical function of the university.

Story-style strategy statements are designed to help people make sense of the university's plans and to provide a deeper sense of meaning and purpose than can be achieved by 'spreadsheet modelling' where data provides the anchor point of the strategy.[2] Their appeal is twofold. First, they rely on the power of storytelling to gain interest and engagement. Second, they present a rosy picture by nearly always glossing over the difficult tasks and hiding the bad bits of the curate's egg. To illustrate this point, consider the strategy statement of the University of Newcastle—'New Futures Strategic Plan 2016–2025'. It highlights the art of Nicole Chaffey, an aboriginal alumnus. Ten full pages of art is showcased. In contrast, the meaty parts of the strategy are relegated to passing reference—two pages are devoted to 'Staff Who Make Their Mark', and there are some scattered references to research. The problem here is that the narrative makes the prominent character in the strategy story a single alumnus while it marginalises staff and research, the two critical aspects of the success of a university.

A second aspect of storytelling is the order in which strategic issues are introduced. We noted three distinct orderings in the narrative statements of strategy. One leads with research, one leads with students and education and one leads with something else, often a social justice theme. For example, the University of Melbourne's statement leads with research. In contrast, the University of Newcastle's statement leads with a social justice theme. Where a university starts, its strategy narrative signals what is most important to the institution. It also anchors its desired reputation position. The University of Melbourne wants to be known as a research institution of excellence. The University of Newcastle wants to be noted for its social justice. Desired reputation is an important strategic consideration because it signals how and where the university will compete for resources. In a knowledge economy research should trump social justice. In a caring economy social justice might trump research. In a regional economy where the University of Newcastle resides it is not clear what role social justice will play in making the institution useful and successful.

A third aspect of storytelling is the language used. Is the strategy presented in plain language; is the language sprinkled with the technical language of strategy; is it presented in an engaging or grand style to evoke interest and emotion? Most statements avoid reference to the language of business and strategy, possibly because it is thought that the reader is unfamiliar with, or may be confused by such language; or just as likely, that corporate language may reflect poorly on the university's public positioning as an inspired institution of research and higher education.

Most statements use a confident and a grand tone of voice, often to the extent that some of their claims resemble 'advertising puffery'. Also, most are populated with photos of some notable people in the academy, ethnically diverse students and the newest or oldest (sandstone) buildings on campus. There is a sameness of these statements to the point where one wonders if they have all been scripted with the help of the same public relations firm. What results is the same story located in a different setting. This speaks to the issue of organisational diversity noted earlier.

Blueprint-style strategies were less evident on university websites. They have a strategic logic that guides linking goals and aspirations to the design and operations of the university. Over the years, academics and management consultants have developed many such frameworks. They help institutions to identify their desired strategic type, conform to it, project a corporate personality and avoid being labelled as 'stuck in the middle' or a 'reactor' to current events.[3] Strategists recognise these frameworks and know their strengths and weaknesses as tools for strategy development. In the public sector some of these are being used to help organisations 'think strategically'.[4]

Blueprint-style strategies often start out by suggesting that Australia's universities are currently experiencing turbulence in their external environment but that the institution will confront these challenges with confidence. To anchor the university against this scenario, most then list their educational mission, vision, values and goals. All want to deliver high-quality learning, be world leaders in research and make a significant contribution to society. All note their programmes are inclusive and accommodate diversity, especially that of indigenous Australians. Again there is an inherent sameness here. In this age of inclusiveness the previous university position of an elite institution providing education for the best and brightest people, and later the professions, is seldom to be found.

To differentiate themselves, some universities highlight their heritage. Others proclaim an enterprise mission. Here, the institution wants to be relevant—to the needs of industry and various sectors of society. Some institutions position themselves as part of an innovation ecosystem. Some position themselves as a model social citizen—a champion of any and every social cause. Regional universities have a slightly different story. They want to be, and be seen as, a key institution in their region—for its cultural and business success.

Somewhere in all the strategy statements, universities have a research story to tell—part of which is factual and part fictitious. The factual part is often illustrated by some notable discoveries or individual awards or the acquisition of significant amounts of funding. Also, many universities now like to claim excellence by stating their ranking in one or more of the numerous reputation polls. The fictitious part of many research stories is that each institution will claim that it is a research powerhouse. Yes, Australia has some of the best researchers in the world in a number of diverse fields, and these people do outstanding work—but there are not very many of these great scholars. And the bigger, sandstone and redbrick universities have most of these (older) scholars. Thus, there are pockets of excellence, not widespread excellence—within and amongst Australia's universities.

Strategically, research is an important issue for Australia and its individual universities. As we will argue later, scientific research, unencumbered by a commercial imperative, is a core capability and provides a competitive advantage for our universities relative to the host of other organisations that conduct research. The type of research done by universities is something that most commercial organisations do not have the time, training or patience to do. The strategic challenge here is that many universities now want to turn some of their research into a revenue stream. As many universities around the world are finding out, this is not an easy endeavour. One reason is that it clashes with a widespread narrative within universities about academic freedom. Another reason is that research that is of interest to, and that will likely be funded by industry, might not generate publications that fit easily into the discipline-based journals that are used by external agencies to rate universities. A third reason is that there are difficulties designing contracts to share the intellectual property rights of the research.

An interesting dilemma exposed by universities trying to monetise research is that industry-focused research often does not address the core issues that give rise to the big, complex issues that confront society. To confront these problems requires extended free time for thinking. For example, consider the Institute for Advanced Study (IAS) located at 1 Einstein Drive, Princeton, New Jersey, USA. The street name gives a clue about the fundamental purpose of this institute, and to its most famous faculty member. IAS is an independent research centre for theoretical research and intellectual inquiry. The faculty have no classes to teach, there are no degree programmes, research is never directed and faculty have no performance goals to meet. IAS has been described as the Celestial Ivory Tower and Intellectual Heaven.[5] This is a place where the big thinkers do the big thinking in mathematics, natural sciences (notably physics), historical studies and social sciences. Australia has a couple of timid versions of IAS.

What is missing from these strategy documents is also noteworthy. Most importantly, there are few hard facts and figures about trends in the operating environment or institutional costs and revenues. Without good data about the institutional environment and the organisation's operations, it is impossible to judge the veracity of the university's goals and aspirations. It is also difficult to describe the business model of the university and to compare it to its local and overseas competitors. With little data, an analyst is forced to scour the university website and its annual reports. And because universities report in different ways, it is difficult and tedious to find information that accurately profiles the university's strategy and then compare one institution against another. So while these are public institutions, they are not transparent institutions.[6]

As noted earlier, a key role of narrative strategy is to get staff and students to buy into and implement, or at least implicitly support, the strategy. So spare a thought for the University of New South Wales in 2019. In an attempt to become more 'global', as its strategy statement loudly proclaimed, it changed its teaching terms from two to three in order to better align its schedule with US universities. Staff and students hated it.[7] So a failure of communication or a poor strategic goal of being 'global' created a significant amount of turmoil on campus.

Our central criticism is that all the strategy statements we could find were incomplete—in ways that signalled that those who crafted these documents were unaware or unconcerned or secretive about some of the most significant aspects of strategy. This is part of the signal sent by the published and public strategy documents. So who is ultimately responsible for sending out such a message? The council of the university.

Notes

1. D. Barry and M. Elmes, "Strategy Retold: Towards a Narrative View of Strategic Discourse", *Academy of Management Review*, Vol. 22, No. 2 (1997), 429–452.
2. See, for example, D. Barry and M. Elmes, "Strategy Retold: Towards a Narrative View of Strategic Discourse", *Academy of Management Review*, Vol. 22, No. 2 (1997), 429–452, and J. Holstein, K. Starkey and M. Wright, "Strategy and Narrative in Higher Education", *Strategic Organization*, Vol. 16, No. 1 (2018), 61–91.
3. For example, universities that focus on research might like to project as maker or innovator or sage. Others that focus more on social justice like to project as humanist or advocate. And if education is the preferred position, then teacher and mentor might be appropriate.
4. See, for example, R. Andrews, G. A. Boyne, J. Law and R. M. Walker, "Strategy, Structure and Process in the Public Sector: A Test of the Miles and Snow Model", *Public Administration*, Vol. 87, No. 4 (2009), 732–749.
5. See, for example, E. Regis, *Who Got Einstein's Office?* (London: Penguin Books, 1987) and https://www.ias.edu
6. This can be compared to a more open governance model in many US universities where external funding demands a different model of accountability and governance. For example, see T. M. Devinney, "Governance at Australian Universities: The Need for a New Model in a World of Capital Raising", at http://www.modern-cynic.org/2013/06/governance/(5 June 2013; accessed 2 August, 2019).
7. K. Prendergast, "No appeasement for UNSW Cancel Trimester Campaign", *Campus Review* (19 June, 2019).

3

University Governance: Weak at the Top

In the romanticised 'golden age' of universities the ivy-clad sandstone buildings formed a sacred site and the beating heart of a university was its tenured scholars. Many people bonded themselves for life to their university. The vice chancellor's door was always open to these scholars. The role of vice chancellor was a part-time appointment occupied by one of the 'older gentleman'. Someone once said that the leader's role was to consider the university to be a rare, delicate, antique crystal bowl. The task was to carry the bowl through a maze of slippery corridors. It didn't matter which corridors were chosen. The only requirement for success was that the vice chancellor must never drop the bowl.

In this world the academics were responsible for the curriculum, student experience and research, while the vice chancellor was responsible for buildings, ceremony and external relations. Heads of departments and faculties defined the direction of their empires and the progress of their academic staff. Many also controlled a discretionary budget for special purposes. In some cases, governance involved a degree of collective decision-making, or at least the sharing of information and the lively discussion of issues that has now largely disappeared from university life.

T. Devinney, G. Dowling, *The Strategies of Australia's Universities*,
https://doi.org/10.1007/978-981-15-3397-6_3

Like an octopus, the university had a small head and many tentacles. By purpose and design it swam through life at a leisurely pace.

In the golden age of the sandstone universities, governance was a scheme where the academic community largely controlled their university through faculty committees and the senate, and where the administration of the university was facilitative and respectful of academic resolutions. The administration of the university was the agent of the academic community. Little wonder that many old academics look back at the previous era with some affection. Today we see the reverse situation where the vice chancellor and his or her executive management team effectively manage the university and the academics are expected to defer to administrative fiat. Now the academics are agents for their university.[1] Because they know no other situation, many young academics simply accept the managerial environment in which they find themselves.

As new public management (NPM) and governance (NPG) ideas invaded the university sector, one outcome has been a transfer of power from various academic committees to the vice chancellor, the senior executive team and often some informal advisory groups (kitchen cabinets) that have no reporting lines or responsibilities to anybody other than the vice chancellor. Members of the executive management team are full-time and well paid, and sometimes motivated by a performance-related bonus.[2] Most appointments are filled through public advertisements with the help of executive search firms rather than from an election within the academy. Many appointees have a non-academic background. One result of this process is that many academics have little empathy for these 'outside' appointments. The executives do not have any moral authority in the institution, especially when they encroach on matters of education and research.

At the faculty level we see that many of these groups are now run by 'manager academics' whose task is to manage up to their 'manager deans', whose task is to manage up to their vice chancellor, whose task is to keep the council informed and confident that he or she is doing a good job. Everybody is an executive in a hierarchy. Deans cease to be academic and discipline leaders. Budgets, often with strings attached, flow down from the level above. Money drifts away from academic groups into special projects.

Today there is little, if any, consultation with academics about the appointment of heads of school and deans, and certainly not for higher-authority positions. Line management from the chancellery has replaced any bottom-up electoral process. Today the notion of a collegial governing or information-sharing environment has been replaced with a hierarchical and often very bureaucratic work environment. This new model of governance is the antithesis of the intellectual equality, openness and participation that define the research practice of most academics. Academics would argue that collegial government is not a sign of complacency, but rather institutional self-confidence in a system that has withstood numerous challenges across the centuries. Also, this is a system that generates its own innovation and leadership. In contrast, the new regime does not recognise and respect internal peer leadership. And, unlike other intellectual capital organisations like professional service firms, university administrators seldom ask their discipline experts for help. Thus the culture of administrators working with their academic colleagues has eroded in many of our public universities.

Time will tell whether or not the current governance regime will help our universities navigate to a sustainable future. A big influence on the likelihood of success will rest on the quality of the strategy developed by the vice chancellor and endorsed by the council. The chair of this august body is the chancellor.

3.1 The Chancellor

The acts and by-laws that establish a university are somewhat vague about the role of a chancellor. Other than preside at meetings, the role of the incumbent seems to be to make good decisions about policy and to support the vice chancellor in the conduct of administering the university.

Chancellors come from a variety of backgrounds, not all of which involve a long relationship with, and deep understanding of universities. Outsiders, however, may bring a fresh mindset to the task of presiding over these large, complex, pluralist organisations. Some chancellors take their position as a community service obligation—it is time to give back to an institution that has probably helped shape their life. Others have a more managerial motivation and may have experience in some major corporations. And some have been long-term academics. Notwithstanding their background, a key requirement is to understand how their big, complex university 'works'. Some chancellors spend much more time and are much more inquisitive than others in this task.

Of the key decisions that reside with the chancellor, by far the most important is the selection of the vice chancellor. The chancellor oversees who is asked to apply and what selection criteria will be used. The key strategic issue here is whether the person is a good fit with the current needs of the university. These needs will be determined in part by the current strategy. In the corporate world there are many examples of CEOs who did not fit with either the culture or the strategic direction of the company they were appointed to. The academic world is no different.

A second key decision, about which we could find little guidance, is the criteria used to assess the performance of a vice chancellor, and what issues might cause the termination of this person. In the corporate world, many of these criteria are transparent, such as meeting expected financial performance targets and managing the risks of business. In a university, while there is accountability to some residual financial indicators, it is unclear what other factors are really important and what factors might lead to the termination of a vice chancellor or other member of the executive team. For example, after James Cook University's unsuccessful prosecution of one of its professors, and the reputation damage that this caused, the vice chancellor held her position.[3]

Another key issue for chancellors is the ongoing working relationship with the vice chancellor. Is the chancellor a mentor and/or supervisor? Does the vice chancellor consider the chancellor and other members of council as subservient to his or her aims? This issue speaks to questions of executive discretion, in particular who has the responsibility for the primary development of university strategy, how will the university be organised to implement the strategy, what criteria will be used to evaluate the strategy and who will be held accountable for its success?

At the heart of the working relationship between a vice chancellor and the council is the information provided to the chancellor and the council about the performance of the institution. Most of it is generated by the senior management team of the university and flows up to the council.

Thus, it is easily filtered and massaged to support the agenda of the vice chancellor. The old BBC comedy series *Yes Minister* and *Yes Prime Minister* cleverly illustrated how organisational information can be shaped to support or contradict any intended decision. It also illustrated how to hide sensitive information in a mass of documents.

Chancellors also have a symbolic role to play. First, their status and reputation prior to joining the university is 'rented' by the university. Thus, they and the other members of council should have exemplary personal reputations. As noted later, in 2018 the reputations of some of Australia's current chancellors (and council members) were tainted during the hearings of the 2018 Australian *Royal Commission into Misconduct in the Banking, Superannuation and Financial Services Industry*. Despite this, these people remained on the councils of universities. A second aspect of symbolism is that the background of the chancellor—such as academic, civil servant, businessperson, scientist or entrepreneur—sends a signal about what is important to the university. This is another aspect of personal reputation, namely, the capability they bring to the job of overseeing the university. Finally, there is the gender and ethnicity of the incumbent. In the era of gender equality we see more women in these roles.

What is interesting about the chancellors of Australia's public universities is that many of these people are almost anonymous. For example, if the University of Technology Sydney wants to be a credible university of technology, then one would expect to see this attribute clearly reflected in the chancellor or some members of the university council. So are there any star technologists on the UTS council? (The university doesn't provide any information about the experience of its members.) Because the University of New South Wales positions itself as a global university, are there any true global citizens on the senate of the university? (The university website doesn't provide any relevant information on this matter.) And because the Australian National University wants to be Australia's national university, are there any national icons on the council of the ANU? The last two chancellors might qualify—both were high-profile federal government foreign ministers. And the current vice chancellor Brian Schmidt might qualify—he is a Nobel laureate.

So how does one become a member of the council of a university? We explore this issue in the following section.

3.2 The Role of the University Council

University councils are essentially a committee of 'grandees' and defenders of university constituencies. We will hereafter call any such top oversight committee the council of the university. This group holds fiscal and legal responsibility for the operations of the university. It is also a 'court of appeal' for both vice chancellors who want to advance a difficult or unpopular cause and disaffected staff who believe the university is heading in the wrong direction or who think that their rights have been harmed. In the NPM era it is an imitative board of directors.

The *Voluntary Code of Best Practice for the Governance of Australian Public Universities* good governance principles specifies that the roles and responsibilities of the council or the equivalent body are:

- Strategic oversight
- Ensuring effective overall management
- Ensuring responsible financial and risk management

These roles and responsibilities mirror those of the boards of many public and private corporations. They focus on 'building tomorrow' (strategy), running today (management) and protecting the institution (risk management). As Robert Scott notes in his book *How University Boards Work*, hopefully a key role of the council is to save the university-of-the-future from the decisions of the day.[4] We see the necessity for this when consulting firms and media commentators decide to pontificate to universities about how they are ill-prepared to embrace the future. Hence, the most effective council members will bring well-informed questions, not fashionable prescriptions.

Another key mindset of many university councils is that success means that nothing bad happens. The role here is to be a safe pair of hands. This defensive attitude relies for its effectiveness on the board's risk-sensing ability. Without meddling too deeply in operational issues (noses in, fingers out), risk-sensing relies on the types and quality of the information passed up the organisation to the board. But what types of information is the council likely to see? The University of Technology 2018 Annual

Report (page 42) suggests that it will relate to 'building projects, environment, health and safety, information technology projects, strategic projects, disaster recovery, emergency management, fraud and corruption, financial risk management, and business continuity planning'. However, what is missing from here are the factors that can ruin a university's academic reputation—like falling and sometimes fraudulent student-entry standards, student misconduct, grade inflation, exploitative employment practices (of part-time teaching and laboratory staff), academic fraud and hysterical (social) media commentary. The academic reputation of a university is just as important as its operational reputation.

Many council members also arrive at meetings with a 'future' mindset. One contrasting pair is to 'do more with less' or 'do more with more'. In the 1970s the governors and top executives of the University of California Berkeley had the first mindset. As state funding decreased, they excelled at devising schemes to maintain quality. In contrast, at Stanford University the mindset was to aggressively seek donations and new sources of funding to improve the university. Both universities progressed but on different pathways and with different internal tensions.[5] Another pair of opposing mindsets is 'to honour the past' or 'embrace agile change'. The first mindset builds on established practices and units of organisation, while the second mindset seeks to reconfigure and rejuvenate the institution. Either can be effective. So a strategic imperative for the chancellors of Australia's public universities is to foster a council mindset that benefits the circumstances of their institution. This is not easy because the composition of the council means that many of its members are appointed to look after the interests of their constituency. Internal disagreement, especially if this becomes public, can derail new ventures, reconfiguration or rejuvenation.

Of particular interest in this book is what is meant by 'strategic oversight'. Does this mean to accept, with or without (minor) modifications, the strategy developed by the vice chancellor and his or her senior management team, or does it mean to help shape this strategy? With the guidance of the chancellor, different councils will inevitably adopt one or other interpretation. Hence, the wisdom of the chancellor is a critical factor in determining the approach that council adopts to reviewing or crafting strategy. However, what we have noticed in many universities is that going on a strategic retreat clearly defines and limits the role of council members. With a busy agenda there is not much time for individuals to delve into the complexity of the institution's proposed new strategy.

3.3 Council Members

The best practice code states that 'apart from the Chancellor, Vice Chancellor and Presiding Member of the Academic Board each member should be appointed or elected. Also, that a council should not exceed 22 members and preferably have no more than 15 members'. For example, the council of the University of New South Wales has three official members (chancellor, president and vice chancellor); president of the academic board (who is elected); five other elected members—two from the academic staff, one from the non-academic staff, two students; and seven appointed members—five appointed by the council and two appointed by the minister. Of the appointed members at least three must be filled by alumni of the university. This structure resembles the supervisory boards of public companies in Germany. Getting them to adopt a specific single mindset will be a challenge.

The Good Governance Code and the governing legislation state that some council members should have 'strong expertise in and knowledge of higher education', 'financial expertise (as demonstrated by relevant qualifications and financial management experience at a senior level in the public or private sector)' and 'commercial expertise (demonstrated by relevant experience at a senior level in the public or private sector)'. Finally, council members should act with common sense, in good faith, with due care and diligence.

One of the key issues missing from this good governance discussion is the role of the ministerial appointments to the council. Is their role as a government appointee to supervise the chancellor and vice chancellor, or is it to help navigate the complexities of government or is it to help protect and enhance the university's budget. As many public US universities have discovered, political appointees often let down their universities as protectors of public funding.

What is also missing from this description of good governance is any mention of required expertise in the first role of the council, namely, strategy. The elected members to council like the academic staff and student representatives are unlikely to have any expertise in strategy. And just because a person has commercial experience doesn't mean that they will have expertise in crafting or reviewing strategy. The problem with commercial experience, as this relates to strategy, is that there are a variety of strategic templates used in commercial settings, and many of these would not migrate well into a university setting.

So, one way to mitigate this problem of a lack of strategy knowledge amongst council members is for the university to appoint people who have seen and been involved in the strategy oversight of a variety of companies. Here the University of New South Wales outpaces most of its peers. At the time of writing, it had six 'professional' directors on its council. Their biographies reveal extensive experience, much of which is current as they are also directors of a variety of profit and non-profit organisations. However, what is somewhat disconcerting is that every council member has another full-time job and that 'Council and Council Committee members serve the University in this way on an entirely voluntary basis'. This means that they have 'no skin in the game' and limited time to do their job. So here we have a complex, billion-dollar-plus university being overseen by a group of busy volunteers fulfilling their community service obligation. While the motives of these council members are honourable, they do not reflect the true nature of what is needed for their position. Good governance requires extensive and informed work from all council members.

Our concern is that many university councils are 'designed to fail' in their task of helping to develop a sound, cohesive and comprehensive strategy for their institution. The depth of expertise required in the council has been designed out of its membership. As we argue later, this is not something that bedevils only university councils.

3.4 The Challenges Faced by Corporate Boards and Councils

The 2018 Australian *Royal Commission into Misconduct in the Banking, Superannuation and Financial Services Industry* exposed the deficiencies of the corporate governance of some of Australia's most prominent financial corporations. From a university perspective what is surprising and disconcerting is that while the Royal Commission was running, the chairs of the boards of the ANZ and Commonwealth Bank of Australia were also the chancellors of two of Australia's universities. And at least three other current council members of Australia's universities (UNSW, UTS and the University of Melbourne) were directors of one of the Big Four banks. The symbolism here is not good. Hopefully, the standards of the university governance will be higher than those of their banks.

An article in the *Australian Financial Review* (2/08/18) and the Australian Broadcasting Corporation's (ABC) *Four Corners* programme 'Money for Nothing' (23/07/18) summed it up well—AMP got into trouble because it was a company with a complicated business model run by some unscrupulous managers who were overseen by an incompetent board. A wonderful irony here is that in the month after this exposé by the ABC its governance was called into question when the board sacked the managing director, and then in the ensuing melee the chair of the board was effectively forced to resign.

In the Australian corporate landscape governance underperformance is widespread. Many of the people appointed to the boards of companies and other organisations are simply not up to the job. There are a number of reasons for this, some of which are also present in university councils, such as:

- *A compromising situation.* Board (council) members are typically invited to join. In the university some are also elected or appointed by a particular constituency. Hence, many invited members will have a strong allegiance to the people who invited them onto the board, and elected and appointed members will be beholden to their constituency.

- *Blind spots.* Most board members have at least one 'blind spot' in their training and experience. Often this is in the areas of finance and strategy. Hence, in discussions involving their blind-spot topic most people will rely on the views of others who they think are more expert than they are. This silent agreement increases the impact of what is said by the person other people defer to. This effectively reduces the number of people on the board and the diversity of knowledge about a particular topic. Hence, a 15-person board will seldom have 15 informed points-of-view on any given topic.
- *Information flows.* Most of the information that arrives in the boardroom is from the managers board members are supposed to be overseeing. You don't have to be a genius to realise how distorted such information can be. And to make matters worse, the sheer volume of material often swamps even the most dedicated board member. Remember in the television series *Yes Minister* how Sir Humphrey always sent his minister home with more reading than he could ever digest. This is a tried and tested tactic to expose but hide crucial information.
- *Board member qualities.* Personal attributes often valued in the boardroom such as collegiality and teamwork can easily lead to groupthink. They also downplay the role of the devil's advocate—to check and challenge ideas put forward by the CEO. Collegiality and teamwork are the antithesis of the wisdom of the crowds approach to good decision-making—where a group of people with separate knowledge assess an issue.
- *Structure.* In Australian boardrooms the push for greater diversity started with making sure that boards were populated by people from different functional areas of business. This is evident in the requirements for university councils. The next phase of extending diversity required demographic or identity or visible diversity—in gender, race, religion, age, disability, sexuality and so forth.[6] However, the problem with these types of diversity is that they are not a substitute for informed insight about the workings of an organisation. A better type of diversity is that of thought and thinking (aka cognitive diversity). When you mix smart, experienced (in the industry), well-informed, critical thinkers together, you are more likely to get some good-quality

thinking than from a group of 'politically-correct diverse' people. Because a by-product of diversity is disagreement, one challenge is to disagree without being disagreeable. A second and more important challenge is for the chancellor to guide the process of decision-making. By this we mean that boards need to learn how to make wise decisions. Slogans like 'learning boards' and 'collaborative boards' recognise this challenge.

- *What to monitor.* While there is common agreement that boards need to focus on corporate (financial) performance, many now also subscribe to a much broader range of goals such as sustainability, social justice and risks associated with climate change and cyber security. There is a much greater degree of agreement in academia and board rooms about how to measure the operational and financial aspects of performance than there is about how to measure something as vague (or slippery) as how an organisation might be exposed to climate change risk. The problem here is that vague goals tend to have vague agendas that tend to be evaluated with vague metrics and often involve vague thinking.
- *Board performance evaluation.* The good governance principles of the *Australian Stock Exchange*, the *Australian Institute of Company Directors* and the *Voluntary Code of Best Practice for the Governance of Australian Public Universities* suggest that boards periodically evaluate their performance. Sounds like a good idea. But who does this? Under the direction of the chancellor of the university the council does this, sometimes with the help of an outside facilitator. But how does a group of people—many of whom self-select each other, who co-create the culture of the group, who create its protocols and who set its agenda—realistically evaluate their own competence and performance? What they will tend to focus on are the hygiene factors of group performance such as how people work together; are meeting agendas organised well; does the chair do a good job of running the meetings; was the last offsite meeting useful; does adequate information flow to the group; is there a good working relationship with the vice chancellor; how useful are the contributions of other members; and so forth. But these factors are seldom the root cause of governance failure. What causes many boards to fail in their responsibilities to the organisation

and its stakeholders is inadequate oversight and incompetence. Without experience and in-depth training in strategy, it is difficult to assess whether the institution's strategy is fit for purpose.

To bring some of these issues together, think about a council meeting where the university's new strategy might be discussed. The chancellor asks the vice chancellor to present and then asks a senior member with strategy experience to lead the discussion. One crucial factor shapes what follows. It is the framework used by the vice chancellor to present the strategy. In most cases this sets the agenda for the following discussion. There will be questions of clarification, requests for more information and statements of agreement and disagreement about certain points, but seldom will anybody directly challenge the structure of the strategy framework used. Unlike some old-fashioned, hard-nosed discussions of research papers, it is an exception for a vice chancellor to be challenged by council members about the strategic framework employed, especially by those elected staff and student representatives who have no strategic competencies. So at best what can be expected is a revise and resubmit, rather than a stress test of the strategy.

Our point in the rest of this book is that if the strategy frameworks used look anything like the statements of strategy published on university websites, they are grossly deficient.

3.5 Developing Strategy

Every few years the council asks the vice chancellor to 'think strategically' and formulate a 5–10-year strategy. This generally involves—forecasting (what the future will look like), some wishful thinking (setting vision and objectives), discovery (auditing the current situation), a wake-up call (what problems do we face), budget modelling (where do we make and spend money), choice (do this but not that) and architecture (this configuration of elements will deliver what we hope to achieve). The published statements of strategy suggest that some build on the previous strategy and are framed as continuing on the same journey, while others seek some disruption with the past and chart a new course. The vice chancellor's introduction in the statement of strategy usually tells this part of the strategy story.

Vice chancellors are important because they are the pivot point for strategy—its formulation, communication and implementation. Their previous history shapes their belief system about how universities work and what template to use to formulate strategy. Those with an academic background are likely to see university strategy differently to those from outside the academy. Academics who have faced (down) large numbers of students and struggled to 'publish or perish' bring a different mindset to what a university is than an outside appointee. They also tend to have a higher degree of 'moral authority' when they ask their academic colleagues to buy into the strategy of the university.

In contrast, a vice chancellor from outside the university often struggles to accommodate the culture of the institution and its sometimes strident professoriate. However, their outside perspective can be helpful in a university system that is becoming more corporatised. A notable example of such a vice chancellor was Fred Hilmer of the University of New South Wales. He did time with the strategy consulting firm McKinsey & Company before becoming dean of the Australian Graduate School of Management (within UNSW), then he became the CEO of Fairfax (the newspaper company) and then back as vice chancellor of UNSW. Under his leadership UNSW sharpened up its strategy—both the process of its creation and the blueprint for guiding the university.

In the corporate world strategy is largely a top-down exercise. The senior management team sets the direction of the company, the board endorses this and everybody else's task is to implement the strategy. A contrasting variation to this process in the university environment is that staff at all levels of the institution may be encouraged to participate in the objective setting phase of strategy development. Possibly because of the lingering idea that universities should be somewhat collegiate, or possibly because it is a social justice idea, there is a tendency for vice chancellors to include an 'ideas forum' in the strategy development process. Staff and (selected) student voices produce a wish list of ideas in isolation of the business model and financial realities of the institution because they are never provided with this information. Also, because you can't have a university-wide ideas forum and then ignore all these suggestions, some need accommodation. As illustrated later, this inevitably involves the expansion of programmes and the adoption of policies to accommodate some special interest group issues. This leads to complexity which manifests itself in a broader footprint for the university, which, in turn, leads to an increase in costs and, subsequently, to seeking new sources of revenue.

3.6 The Fish Thinks from the Head[7]

One of our major concerns about the councils of many Australian public universities is structural in nature. Like many corporate boards, university councils are easily led by their vice chancellor (here is the new strategy for comment), and often lack the skills to evaluate this strategy because the distribution of relevant expertise amongst the council is limited to only a few members. Add to this that the work expectations of their members limit the amount of time available to deep-dive into key aspects of the strategy, and we see a system that is 'designed to fail'.

Another issue is that the composition of a council is designed to reflect stakeholder self-interest. For example, in the UNSW Council there are really only five independent members. Realistically what can only be expected from the elected staff, student representatives and the nominated political appointees is to look out for the interests of their constituencies. For example, Cissy Shen, a student representative on the Macquarie University governing body, stated in her bio that she 'wants Macquarie University as a place that puts students first'. Also, do we really believe that a staff member who is supportive of the staff union will act in the best interests of the university if the strategy suggests any degradation of working conditions?

One way to mitigate the constituent focus of some council members would be to require all members to subscribe to a Code of Conduct that specified their responsibilities—first to the university, second to the university's stakeholders, third to Australia and fourth to the rest of the world. One of our colleagues, Roger Collins, suggested that governance groups like this face two types of decision situations—square-table decisions are made when people push the agenda of their constituency, while round-table decisions are made when the interests of the organisation as a whole are paramount. All council decisions should be made at a round table—literally and figuratively.

Finally, even though many council members are (elected) volunteers, those without relevant experience should be required to upgrade their strategic thinking skills. Professional board members regularly do this, so why not university council members.

Notes

1. C. Lorenz, "If You're So Smart, Why Are You under Surveillance? Universities, Neoliberalism, and New Public Management", *Critical Inquiry*, Vol. 38 (2012), 599–629.
2. For example, university annual reports tabled in the NSW State Parliament indicated that in 2011 professor Stephen Schwartz of Macquarie University received bonuses totalling $462,240 in a total salary of $1,184,661; professor Michael Spence of the University of Sydney received a performance bonus of $167,432 out of his salary of $911,575; and Professor Fred Hilmer of UNSW received $847,599 with no bonuses.
3. J. Albrechtsen, "Wrong head rolled over a uni blue still smouldering", *The Australian* (25–26 May, 2019), p. 26.
4. R. Scott, *How University Boards* Work (Baltimore, Maryland: John Hopkins University Press, 2018).
5. Reported in S. Leih and D. Teece, "Campus Leadership and the Entrepreneurial University: A Dynamic Capabilities Perspective", *Academy of Management Perspectives*, Vol. 30, No. 2 (2016), p. 199.
6. This often leads to what is known as the Noah's Ark solution, whereby as the Good Governance Code referred to notes, that the council should have one of those, two of those and some of those.
7. The saying "the fish rots from the head" was made popular by B. Garratt, *The Fish Rots from the Head: The Crisis in our Boardrooms: Developing the Crucial Skills of the Competent Director* (London: Profile Books, 2003).

4
What Is Strategy?

The word strategy is derived from the Greek word strategos or 'the art of the general'. Thus, the origin of the word puts the responsibility for strategy at the top of an army/business/university. But as noted in Chap. 3, university generals (chancellors) seem to be leading as much from behind their CEOs (vice chancellors) as in front of them.

To evaluate a strategy first requires specifying what strategy is. Here our working description is that strategy is the whole pattern of decisions that set the long-term direction of the university. As with any set of decisions, some are more important than others. These are the ones that require major or irrevocable commitments of resources. And as with any pattern, a critical concern is the coherence of decisions over time and over the functions and domains of the organisation that collectively create value for stakeholders.

For Australia's universities strategy ranges over functions and operational units. The principal functions are research, education and engagement. The principal units are the various faculties (or schools and research centres) and administrative/operational units of the university. Hereafter we will call the university's collection of decisions corporate strategy, functional strategy and business unit strategy. Figure 4.1 shows how they

T. Devinney, G. Dowling, *The Strategies of Australia's Universities*,
https://doi.org/10.1007/978-981-15-3397-6_4

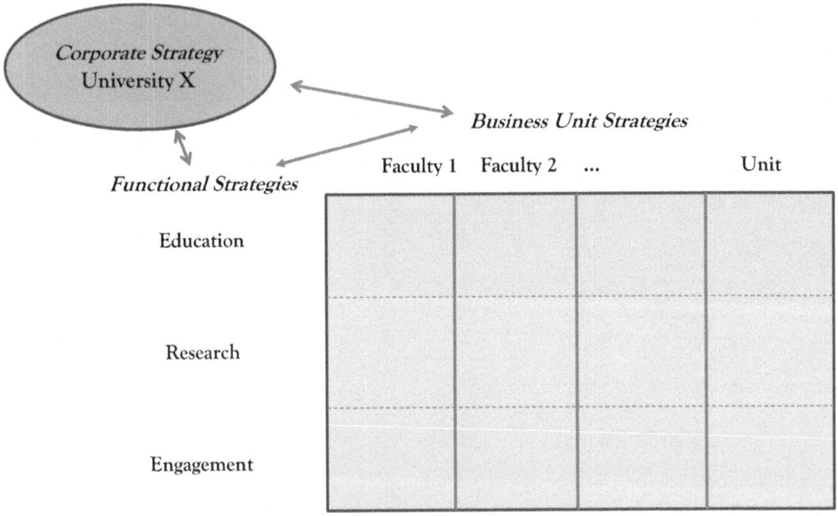

Fig. 4.1 Different types of strategy

relate to each other. By relationship we mean that the various strategies depend on, or add value to, each other to deliver the university's chosen objectives, which are discussed in detail in Chap. 7.

While this book deals mostly with corporate strategy, it will occasionally refer to the other two types of strategy. In fact, an Internet search using the phrase 'university strategy' will find examples of all three strategies. What is interesting and insightful about many of these functional and business unit strategy statements is that they seldom talk directly to each other. (We return to this issue later.)

4.1 Strategy Framework

Donald Hambrick and James Fredrickson's strategy framework is used to guide the following discussion of corporate strategy. It is used in many courses taught in business schools. So in keeping with the principle of doing what is taught in the classroom, here is an overview of their framework.

1. Review the environment in which the institution operates.
2. Specify the mission or vision of the university—its fundamental purpose (telos) and values.

   Phase 1 and 2 guide the choice of
3. Objectives—specific targets. These should focus on running today, building tomorrow and protecting the institution. From these it should be clear what the university wants to do and will not do.

   Objectives then guide the university's
4. Strategy—the central, integrated, externally oriented concept (and collection of decisions) of how the university will achieve its objectives.

   Strategy dictates what supporting
5. Organisational arrangements are necessary to implement the strategy and achieve the stated objectives.

We note that this five-phase, linear outline is oversimplified. In practice, strategy formulation is often a messy process. While it involves these steps, it inevitably involves iterating backwards and forwards through this process. However, for the sake of exposition, and as an outline for reviewing the strategy of Australia's universities, it serves its purpose well.

This simple outline specifies that strategy starts with an assessment of the environment in which a university operates. This will include any factor that is likely to intrude on the evolutionary fitness of the university. By this we mean the political, economic, social and technological forces that shape the world of higher education. The university's mission needs to reflect what the institution's major stakeholders expect from it. As noted earlier, the Grand Bargain is a key factor here.

Next, a university's objectives need to reflect the environment and mission of the university. As we will discuss in Chap. 8, there is a tension here between objectives that are realistic and those that are fanciful. Next strategy involves specifying the 'central concept' of the university. At a recent strategy launch event one of Australia's vice chancellors stated that the central concept of his university was 'transforming to lifetime learning'. While these words hovered over his head on the big screen, he explained this idea as moving the university from a batch-processing model of education to a continuous production or life-long learning model of education. Finally, strategy implementation requires choosing

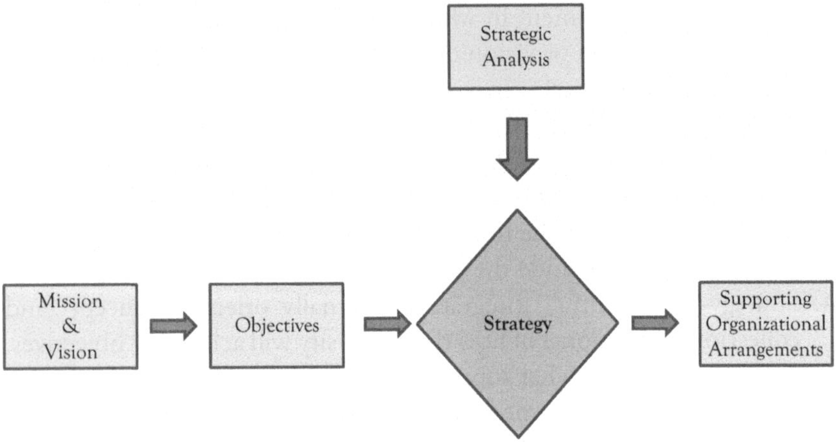

Fig. 4.2 Putting strategy in its place

how the university will be organised. As Chap. 11 notes, this is a major issue for most universities.

Figure 4.2 puts strategy in its place and is reproduced from Hambrick and Fredrickson's paper. While this also has a sequential nature, because most strategies tend to emerge and evolve as the organisation goes along, many of these elements may occur simultaneously.

The key point in Fig. 4.2 is that Mission and Vision (such as 'we aim to be great') and Objectives ('we will be ranked in the top 100') are not strategies—they are guides to strategy. Also, strategy is not a description of the Supporting Organizational Arrangements (such as 'we have 2,000 staff organized into 6 faculties and 23 schools where we offer 166 degrees'). Unfortunately, it is these three types of information that pervade the strategy statements of most of our universities.

Hambrick and Fredrickson suggest that the key elements of an organisation's strategy are:

- *Arenas*—where the university will operate: which faculties, courses, research areas, type of students and so forth. In Fig. 4.1 these choices and investments will be found in the university's corporate strategy. Operational choices will be a business unit (faculty) strategy responsibility.

- *Vehicles*—how the university will deliver its education and produce research: for example, through a particular type or mix of educational technologies (aka EdTech), research infrastructure, engagement partnerships and so forth. Many of these choices and investments will be found in the university's functional strategies.
- *Differentiators*—how the university will be meaningfully different to attract target staff and students: for example, through things like its location, buildings, campus life, employment contacts, accreditation, student scholarships. These decisions will be found in the corporate and functional strategies.
- *Staging*—the speed and sequence of major activities needed to increase the likelihood of success: such as broadening or shrinking the range of course offerings, expanding geographically, investing in advertising and brand building, investing in new learning technologies, opening new buildings. This is the domain of corporate and functional strategies.
- *Economic Logic*—how the university's fundamental and relatively enduring capabilities enable it to be economically sustainable: for example, by growing to achieve better economies of scale, by building reputation to stimulate demand and support premium prices, by offering a better level of quality education at a similar price to competitors; by commercialising teaching and research. This is the domain of corporate strategy.

These elements of strategy are shown in Fig. 4.3. They all require choice and investment and alignment. Getting this right is what makes strategy such a difficult task. And it is the coupling—or as strategists like to say,

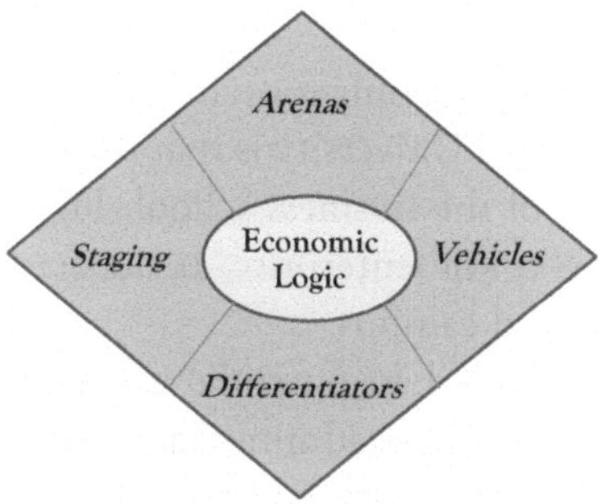

Fig. 4.3 The five major elements of strategy

the 'fit' of these elements—that makes imitation by competitors difficult. Therefore, two universities might look the same but one might have a much better strategy than the other.

Figure 4.3 positions the economic logic of the university as the anchor point of strategy. The role of the other elements is to underwrite this business model, and thus the revenues and costs of the university. And here is a crucial limitation of every statement of strategy of Australia's universities that we could find. None of them related all the fragments of their strategy to the economic logic of the institution. At our last university some of this was done through the annual budgeting process, which is called the corporate plan. The problem here is that this type of information is only available to internal staff. Without seeing how strategic decisions impact costs and revenues, it is impossible to gauge the viability and long-term sustainability of a strategy.

The World's Most Profitable Mini-university

To illustrate the overall logic of Fig. 4.3, consider what is arguably the most profitable part of one of the world's most respected universities, namely, the Harvard Business School (HBS). This school is really a mini-university that trades under the umbrella brand of Harvard University. In 2015 it had revenues of US$707million, which makes it the size of a mid-size Australian university. It is, and has been for decades, ranked amongst the top business schools in most international rankings. It is extremely wealthy and highly successful. However, it is very controversial as an exemplar of academic quality. Notwithstanding this, it remains the poster child of business schools.

- *University Governance*—the only formal relationship between the business school and Harvard University is that the president of the university selects the dean of the business school. HBS is a 'float your own boat' or 'eat what you kill' enterprise. It sits across the Charles River from the main Harvard campus.
- *Arenas*—bring the world's best potential general managers to HBS for an MBA (master of business administration) degree. Select students that will contribute to the culture of the school's learning (because of their previous work experience) and who will be easily employable

after graduation. Then help these students get better jobs than they had previously in leading corporations around the world. Bring managers of organisations to one of the HBS short-course executive development programmes, and then send them back to their companies with the HBS Good Housekeeping seal of approval.

- *Vehicles*—internally develop a suite of corporate case studies to use in the classroom. Fund a programme to keep these relevant. Invite leading CEOs to address students. Recruit academics who are great teachers (and train those who are not) and who are comfortable researching and advising major corporations. To keep up the institution's academic credibility, hire some star scholars. Get leading academics and practitioners to write for the *Harvard Business Review*. Invest in outstanding infrastructure (new and beautiful old buildings) and sufficient accommodation on campus to create a 'sacred site' experience. To bond the students, form them into class sections where each group forms its own identity and must learn to work together. Have the alumni office keep in touch with graduates, and help them keep in touch with each other to cement their experience and recommend the business school. Facilitate the biggest and best companies and professional service firms coming to campus to recruit.
- *Differentiators*—HBS case studies have a distinct format. Being taught with these case studies is a unique experience. Harvard Business School is a special place for those who attend; it is expensive and somewhat exclusive for students and academics. Develop a strong brand image and make sure it is different to the other great Boston business school—the Sloan School at MIT, and its West Coast rival, Stanford University.
- *Staging*—keep academics, courses and teaching material up to date and relevant to new and emerging business conditions. Have people come to the HBS campus, because this helps to support the teaching and accommodation that are priced at a premium. Don't allow the Internet distributed learning technology to erode the social and psychological value of 'going to Harvard Business School'. Use social (business) media and events to help alumni maintain relationships with members of their cohort (class section and year). Use the *Harvard Business Review* magazine to keep the name and profile of the business school prominent.

- *Economic Logic*—this is an expensive operation to run, so charge premium prices, load up the volume of students and capitalise on the efficiency of replication by repeating the big money-earning courses. Commercialise teaching by selling the school's case studies to other business schools. Sell management thought-leader insights to academics and practicing managers through the school's publishing house—books, blogs and the *Harvard Business Review*. Have the alumni office ask for financial and other types of support for the school. Encourage the academics to consult to big business, because this helps to develop new case studies, build closer relationships with industry, and defray some of the costs of employing the best academics.[1]

Duff McDonald, in his unflattering book *The Golden Passport*, suggests that the school's core strategic concept is to be an educational institution and job placement service, plus a networking facilitator for many of the world's business leaders.[2] From the perspective of the student, it is a boot camp for business. For companies and professional service firms that recruit from the school, it is a screening service. And for companies that send their managers to its executive programmes it is a finishing school. Industry engagement is the overriding mission of the business school. It has been very financially successful in this enterprise.[3] It has also been enormously influential in educating a large cohort of managers who run and direct many of the world's largest corporations, sometimes for the benefit of society and sometimes to its detriment.[4] The former US president George W. Bush is an alumnus.

4.2 The University and Its Faculties

A key aspect of university strategy is the relationship between the faculties (business unit) and the central administration of the university. As Donald Sull and his colleagues note, these relationships will define a key part of the logic of a conglomerate-style institution's corporate strategy.[5] Let's describe their line of thinking as it applies to a university.

The faculties of a university can be related or unrelated to each other and to the central administration of the institution. The central administration (corporate core) of the university has both a design and a parenting role to play here. Sull and his colleagucs advocate modelling these design choices by defining two types of relationship. One is how reliant the faculties are on one another to deliver their education and research. The other relationship is how reliant the faculties are, or should be, on the central administration's resources and capabilities. Figure 4.4 illustrates the possibilities.

There are four broad logics in Fig. 4.4. Looking at each academic unit and placing it into one of the quadrants suggests how the university is currently organised to meet its mission and objectives. The strategic question here is whether the pattern of faculty placement is suitable to achieve the university's goals. While the mix of faculties for each university will differ, the strategic question remains the same. To populate the model, consider the following example.

- The Leverage logic indicates that there will be some faculties that have to make heavy use of the resources and services of the university to survive. For example, many arts and pure mathematics faculties can only exist if they draw on pooled university revenue. These faculties will also use the central services of the university to access supporting infrastructure.

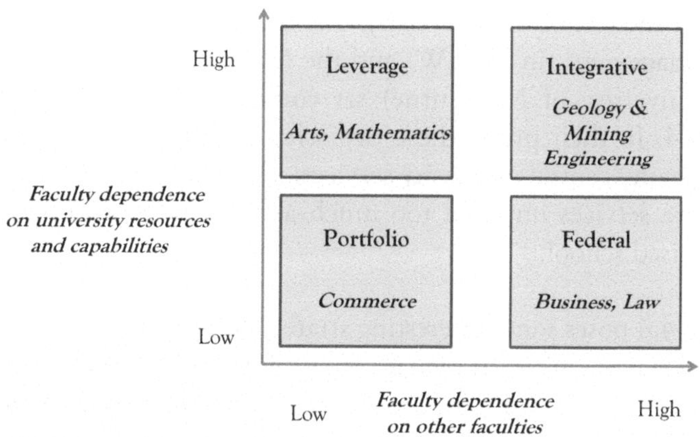

Fig. 4.4 Alternative strategic logics

- The Integrative logic indicates that some faculties will rely on university resources and services, and they will benefit by creating strategic alliances with other faculties. For example, small faculties like geology and mining engineering, neither of which may be self-sustaining, can benefit from working together.

The next two logics focus on faculties that don't need much support from central administration. Many professional schools fit this description because they are often competent in running their own operations. Also, the demand for their courses and research provides adequate funding to operate.

- The Portfolio logic indicates that it is useful to gather up marginally related disciplines in a single school. For example, many large faculties of commerce are really portfolios of marginally related disciplines. They are composed of separate departments of accounting, economics, finance, management, marketing, human resources, information science, operations and occasionally statistics. Different combinations of these disciplines are packaged as different degrees under the broad umbrella of a 'business education'. However, seldom do these disciplines join together in teaching a specific subject or researching a particular issue.
- The Federal logic contains faculties that are or wish they were independent of the rest of the university. The old Australian Graduate School of Management (in UNSW) and the Melbourne Business School (in the University of Melbourne) sat comfortably in this quadrant of Fig. 4.4. In their prime these two schools deliberately tried to avoid using many central university services. The whole-of-university nature of these services imposed too much administrative complexity on a specialised school.

Figure 4.4 poses some interesting strategic questions, such as, should a university have faculties in each quadrant or would it be better to have all the faculties in one quadrant, or one row, or column of the matrix? If a university has faculties in every quadrant like the profile in Fig. 4.4, it suggests that the institution has four competing strategy logics. Hence, the task of designing and getting commitment to a single corporate strategy will be difficult. Another key strategic issue motivated by Fig. 4.4 and discussed extensively in the following chapters is whether a university should foster a cross-subsidy (leverage and integrative) or an internal privatisation (portfolio & federal) approach to organisation, governance and budgeting. Given the importance of these two questions, it is strange that they are seldom, if ever, mentioned in a university's public statement of strategy.

An organisational culture issue that is signalled by Fig. 4.4 is the motivation for a faculty to help other faculties in the university portfolio. For example, because of strong student demand and the relatively low costs of business education and research, many business schools are profit centres within the university. If they were able to keep and reinvest these profits, they could easily become high-quality self-sustaining entities. When these faculties are highly taxed to support other parts of the university, their staff and students have a claim to be rewarded for acting as the institution's automatic teller machine (ATM). Seldom is this role openly discussed by the central administration, and it is never recognised in the statements of strategy found on the Internet. We return to this issue in Chap. 8 when we discuss the economics of a university.

From a parenting perspective, if the value of a university is to be greater than the sum of its parts, central administration needs a strategy for adding value to the faculties and the institution as a whole. It does this by providing operational support for the faculties, such as back-office human resources and information technology; basic services for teaching and research, such as student recruitment and research support; university buildings and infrastructure maintenance, and by managing key external stakeholders like government, workplace unions and alumni. However, a sound parenting strategy is more than just a collection of operational activities. It needs to add value by making investments in university-wide assets like fund raising, campus improvements and building the institution's reputation. And beyond these activities, a good parent will provide direction to its faculties via strategic planning, process improvement, performance monitoring and directing cooperation amongst faculties along the lines noted in Fig. 4.4.

As noted in Chap. 11, most of Australia's universities make no mention of how their faculties relate to each other or to the central administration. They are simply listed on the institution's organisation chart as separate entities that report up through the hierarchy eventually to the vice chancellor. Hence, these organisation charts are 'strategy-free' in the sense that while they might help somebody identify key parts of the bureaucracy, they don't provide any information about the importance of faculties, their relationship to each other or how the university might bestow favours or allocate resources.

4.3 The University and Its Functions

The final part of Fig. 4.1 is the university's functional strategies—education, research and engagement. In the past the strategy narrative was a nebulous notion of how a university education contributes to civil society, and how teaching and research mysteriously create economic prosperity or more informed citizens. Today the general narrative in strategy statements is that the relevance of education is to gain a (worthwhile) job and prepare students for life and leadership. The relevance of research is to shape policy and drive discovery and innovation in the knowledge economy. The relevance of engagement is to link with industry (to signal relevance and gain their financial support) and the local community (to be seen as a good neighbour and offer support to various groups). What is disappointing is that most discussions of teaching, research and engagement are plagued with banalities.

From a strategy perspective, functional strategies need to have a clear internal logic and be clear about how they combine to support the overall corporate strategy. A recent statement by the vice chancellor of the Australian National University (ANU) illustrates this challenge.[6] Brian Schmidt believes that a great university is first made by its students. On the university website he describes the ANU's education strategy—it will limit the size of the student cohort to around 9500 undergraduates and a similar number of postgraduates. This is the best balance for the university. It will have critical mass across its study areas and human-size cohorts of students so that they get to know their teachers and classmates. Teachers will be active researchers. Classmates will come from diverse backgrounds. Because students learn best when they learn actively, courses and learning spaces will be designed accordingly. To create an experience that is as enriching as possible, the university will provide every student with the opportunity to live on campus and to extend their thinking beyond their chosen discipline of study. And because the ANU is the national university with a global mission, it will recruit the best students from every school in Australia and use scholarships to make it easy for these students and similar others from around the world to attend the ANU. What is interesting is that all of the Group of Eight Australian universities have a similar education strategy—to seek the best and brightest students and provide them with a rich and rewarding educational experience.

A problem with the functional strategies of many universities is that they are underdeveloped. For example, a university-wide education strategy needs a university-wide personnel strategy to ensure the correct mix of teacher-research academics. It also needs relevant individual and group-based key performance metrics that are aligned with desired outcomes. It needs performance development and appraisal systems plus salary and promotion criteria that support these outcomes. At the university level we could seldom find a coherent personnel strategy for the total cohort of academic employees. Universities know how many people of different grades they have and how much they are paid. They even know the names and accomplishments of some of their star teachers and researchers. But they generally don't know the distribution of quality and capabilities of their workforce across the institution. For this type of information they tend to rely on the opinions of their (manager) faculty deans.

Another problem is that the interactions between research, education and engagement are often underdeveloped. Seldom does a statement of strategy identify the factors that facilitate interaction across the functions. Later we will identify some cases where operational procedures actually work against functional excellence and interaction. We refer to this issue as 'hoping for A while rewarding B'.

University annual reports also discuss the primary functions of the university. However, these are generally in separate sections. So again the relationships amongst functions are only partially recognised or articulated. This is lamentable because in a study looking at UK university bureaucracy, Rhys Andrews and his colleagues suggest that the strength of the intellectual climate of a university (as measured by its research performance) benefits both research and teaching.[7] Also, in our experience as business school professors we often saw these spillovers go the other way—from executive teaching to research. The experience that executives and MBA students brought to classroom discussions often triggered latter research enquiry. So there are positive spillovers between research and education and engagement. (Hence, the dashed horizontal lines in Fig. 4.1.)

Figures 4.1, 4.2, 4.3 and 4.4 provide a template to assess the coverage and thus comprehensiveness of a university's strategy. All the pieces need to be present and organised to form a coherent and compelling strategy. This is the art of the general. They also need to be communicated so that employees and outside stakeholders know why things have happened and what to expect. This is the task of narrative strategy. When things are missing, the strategy is incomplete, and it encourages people within the organisation to fill in the blanks.

As an observation Hambrick and Fredrickson note, 'most strategic plans emphasise one or two of the elements without giving any consideration to the others' (p. 54). And this is the major weakness of all the published strategies of Australia's (and many overseas) universities.

Notes

1. Much of this consulting is done on the private account of the academic.
2. D. McDonald, *The Golden Passport* (New York: Harper Business, 2017).
3. For example, McDonald (p. 533) notes that in 2015 the school serviced more than 10,000 managers through 79 executive education programmes to raise $168 million. Also, the publishing division made $203 million. MBA tuition and fees raised $120million. A further $216 million came from endowment distributions, gifts and housing rents. And at this time its endowment was $3.3 billion.

4. A large part of this success has come from its strategic alliance with the management consulting firm McKinsey & Company who recruited heavily from the school. One writer called this alliance *McHarvard*.
5. D. Sull, S. Turconi, C. Sull and J. Yoder, "Four Logics of Corporate Strategy, *MIT Sloan Management Review*, Vol. 59, No. 2 (2018), 136–142.
6. Brian Schmidt, "A great university is first made by its students". From http://www.anu.edu.au/news/all-news/a-great-university-is-first-made-by-its-students.
7. R. Andrews, G. Boyne, and A. M. S. Mostafa, "When Bureaucracy Matters for Organizational Performance: Exploring the Benefits of Administrative Intensity in Big and Complex Organizations", *Public Administration*, Vol. 95, No. 1 (2017), 115–139.

5

Strategic Frameworks

Because any discussion of the strategy of an organisation generally involves reference to various frameworks and specific concepts, here are some that we will use throughout the remainder of this book. As Donald Siegel and Sohvi Leih state in their editorial to the special issue of strategic management for universities, such frameworks are useful as lens through which to identify problems, evaluate various aspects of strategy and judge if it will deliver a sustainable future.[1] Also, it is this language of the discipline that is largely missing from the published statements of strategy refereed to throughout this book.

5.1 Business Models

Business model is a term used by strategists in different ways. Some use it as a framework similar to the value chain in Fig. 7.1 (in Chap. 7) for describing the set of integrated activities for making something and selling it. Other people use the term as a theory of firm value creation, and others use it as a catchphrase about how the organisation works to deliver value to its target customers. For example, as a business theory for Apple,

T. Devinney, G. Dowling, *The Strategies of Australia's Universities*,
https://doi.org/10.1007/978-981-15-3397-6_5

the late Steve Jobs held that consumers would pay a premium for ease of use, reliability and elegance in computing and personal digital devices. The best means to deliver these customer benefits was by controlling design, building products with proprietary integrated hardware and software systems, and identifying, branding and controlling complementary products (like iTunes). He once described this as making tools for the mind that advance humankind.

Some companies try to summarise their business model in a catchphrase or by-line. For example, the retailer Costco's business model can be described as 'pile it high and sell it cheap'. The old Amazon business model was 'get big fast and hope that the winner takes all'. The old BHP business model was 'dig and deliver'. The luxury department store Harrods business model is 'rely on the natural instincts of its merchants about taste and style'. Those television shows that feature farmers that grow their own produce and then use this in their own restaurant often describe their business model as 'from paddock to plate'. And some pharmaceutical companies describe their business as 'from bench to bedside'.

Some potential university business models are: education on demand (say, via e-learning technology), workforce education (like the University of Phoenix), discover to educate (which is what MIT claims), from cooks (undergraduates who follow a recipe) to chefs (postgraduates who create new recipes) and the best inputs (school-leavers) create the best outputs (graduates). As snappy as many such descriptions are, they hide the fact that a university has two fundamental business models. One is the creation of new knowledge via research, and the other is the dissemination of old and new knowledge via education. Operationally a university divulges most of the responsibility for both functions to its faculties. This is why every strategy should be clear about the capabilities of these 'business units'. It should also be clear about how the central administration 'parents' the faculties and adds value to their operations. As we note later, the economic roles, resourcing, management and reputations of the portfolio of faculties are key strategic issues. However, seldom does a statement of strategy contain this vital information.

5.2 Economies of Scale, Scope and Focus

In strategy jargon, an organisation can achieve a cost advantage, or in the case of universities, greater efficiency, by better utilising its assets and other resources—economies of scale. For example, a university could better utilise its buildings, IT systems and academics by running courses every day of the year (well maybe not on public holidays). At the old Australian Graduate School of Management (AGSM), while the MBA programme followed the university teaching calendar, executive short-courses were used to fill in much of the between-term slack periods—even weekends. These courses typically started classes at 8.30 a.m. and concluded at 9 p.m., with breaks for meals and class preparation. The course director was with the students from 7 a.m. (breakfast) to 10 p.m. (evening drinks after class) every day.[2]

A second source of cost efficiency arises because of the ability to spread production and service technologies across products, and leverage intangibles such as a respected brand name—economies of scope or synergies. Consider the AGSM again. The MBA brand name is well known as a particular type of education that is attractive to a particular type of student. Thus, the MBA brand reduces the overall costs of marketing to the targeted full-time, part-time and executive students. The research done to create courses for the MBA programme is also used to create courses for the shorter executive programmes. Many of the case studies used in the MBA programme and the executive short courses were the same. The real-world examples of business practice that were discovered from participants in the executive programmes were later used in the MBA programme to illustrate industry relevance. Research involving data from Australian companies would be published in academic papers and used in both programmes. So the set-up costs of a business topic could be amortised over multiple programmes. Economies of scope are much easier to achieve if there is a commonality of interest, such as in this example of designing a set of integrated courses about general management.

Another source of cost advantage comes from accumulated experience. As individuals and organisations gain experience with a task, they generally become more efficient doing that task. In a university setting we see this in the efficiencies of more experienced teachers, researchers and administrators. They make fewer mistakes and they are quicker to get things done. So the mix of experienced and novice staff is important to manage. Few universities seem to acknowledge this source of efficiency. In contrast, in the AGSM there were many more professors and associate professors than in a typical Australian university faculty. There were two reasons for this. One was the efficiency effect just noted. The other was a signal of quality—high-fee-paying students wanted service from experienced academics.

Finally, there is the efficiency gained from economies of focus—the notion of less is more. The AGSM was a graduate school with a limited range of programmes (doctoral programme, full-time and executive MBA, and executive programmes that borrowed from the courses in the MBA). The coursework programmes were targeted at an easily identified group of students—continuing managers, some of whom were supported by the companies they worked for. The total number of students was small by Australian university standards. The school sought academics who had a common interest in business, who could teach and research together and who could teach across different programmes. The school was a highly focused niche operation within the University of New South Wales. From a strategic perspective the AGSM was an example of a unit of the university 'that floated its own boat', a Federal faculty in Fig. 4.4. That is, it was largely self-sufficient and autonomous. Many of the best business schools of the world have this character.

Because it lacked economies of scale, the AGSM strategy was built on economies of scope and focus—the school's resources were utilised more than most of those in a traditional university, and many activities cross-fertilised each other more than could be achieved in a typical Australian university. Later in its life the AGSM was merged with the much larger faculty of economics and commerce to become part of the Australian School of Business. Here, the search was for economies of scale.

What is interesting about the statements of strategy of Australia's public universities is the almost complete lack of discussion of anything other than economies of scale through the growth of (international) students. The underlying philosophy here seems to be 'bigger is better' or 'more is more'. However, there are some universities like the California Institute of Technology and the London School of Economics, many professional service firms and many businesses that have built great reputations by being focused. So the strategic question arises as to the optimum size and design for a public university in the Australian higher education system, especially one in the major cities where a number of universities co-locate.

Our observation is that a typical Australian university thinks that it needs to be bigger to do more. Our contrarian response is that a university does not need to be bigger to be better. We return to this issue later.

5.3 Comparative and Competitive Advantage

Comparative advantages are situation-specific advantages that competitors can replicate at a reasonable cost by relocating or by altering the situational circumstances. That is, they are temporary. For example, some years ago one of Australia's universities decided to advertise at a major sporting event. It was not long until other universities advertised at similar sporting events, such as major rugby union games, golf championships and tennis tournaments. The comparative advantage, if any, of this new advertising campaign was nullified.

Competitive advantages are organisational-specific advantages that cannot be imitated by competitors or can only be mimicked at a very high cost. For example, what universities do better than most commercial organisations is take the time to do research at a higher standard of scientific integrity than these corporations. They employ people with the best training, conflicts of interest are minimal, and the peer-review process helps to ensure that what gets published has been vetted by external peers. This type of slow, deliberate research is their competitive advantage relative to commercial firms. In contrast, the competitive advantage of commercial firms is developmental research where basic research is translated into business process improvements and product and service innovations.

When universities venture into the realm of developmental research, they need to tread carefully. For example, university management systems that focus on academic integrity are often not well suited to getting researches to adhere to the requirements of a commercial environment. Hence, rather than push academics to do more applied research, one strategy is to harness the entrepreneurial instincts of some of the students and encourage a new business start-up culture. The role of the academics here is to guide and encourage this cohort. The challenge is to capture some of the rents from the basic research that underpins these new ventures.

A competitive advantage for some Australian universities relative to their peers is their location close to an industrial group or a natural resource or a research hot spot. For example, James Cook University sits beside the Great Barrier Reef, which as a world heritage site provides many research opportunities. Hence, marine science should be, and is, a speciality for the university. In comparison, the University of Newcastle sits beside one of the largest coal mining and exporting regions in the world and a major air-force base (Williamstown), and it is close to one of Australia's premier wine-growing regions (the Hunter Valley). One might expect that these three locational assets would spur the university to have major programmes that specialise in the research and educational opportunities these locational advantages offer. A look at the university website suggests only small pockets of expertise.

Other competitive advantages are permanent until disrupted by innovations that create a significantly better value proposition for the target customers of the university. For example, the reputations of Oxford and Cambridge Universities encapsulated in their Oxbridge approach to higher education have provided these institutions with an advantage over their local and many overseas universities. So far, this approach to education has withstood many new educational technologies. Also, the alumni networks of these universities provide a substantial advantage in attracting academics, students, benefactors and visitors that further enrich these UK institutions.

Two things are important about comparative and competitive advantages. First, they are defined relative to competitors. Second, they are not necessarily independent or separable. Hence, the total advantage of a university is not simply the sum of its comparative and competitive advantage. It is also important to note that a university can have comparative and competitive disadvantages. For example, the university union–negotiated modest academic salaries and the high cost of living in Australia's big cities have discouraged many overseas star academics from joining an

Australian university. Also, a poorly functioning admission and registration system can discourage good students from joining a university.[3]

When discussion focuses on comparative and competitive advantage, the next step is to consider sustainable advantage. These are the advantages that management can strengthen, extend into the future and extend across product offerings. They often arise from innovation (a new or different solution to a problem), capacity and cost position (gaining economies of scale), segmentation (a better understanding of student or industry needs) and time (doing things faster). The MOOCs—the Massive Open Online Courses—are an example of this. These courses use innovation, a new knowledge delivery mechanism; segmentation, to reach some traditional and new segments of students; time, to deliver information to students when they want to receive it;and capacity, once a course is established it costs almost nothing for extra students to access it. This is why MOOCs are concerning some universities. Because of their potential disruptive influence on the business model of universities, we will analyse these in the next section.

5.4 Sustaining Versus Disruptive Innovation

In 1997 Clayton Christensen, a professor at the Harvard Business School, wrote a book titled *The Innovator's Dilemma*. This book consists of a set of hand-picked case studies from which he argues that the dilemma organisations face is that by doing the right thing—improving what they are currently doing (sustaining innovation)—they are doing the wrong thing, because they are not seeking to radically innovate and create new markets (disruptive innovation). The first problem with this theory is that it is built on a set of hand-picked anecdotes—a notoriously weak methodology.[4] A second problem is that it largely ignores how the history of an organisation creates a set of enduring commitments to its stakeholders that are very difficult to ignore. Organisations can't expect to prosper by walking away from their current stakeholders or asking them to radically change their behaviour. Notwithstanding these shortcomings, Christensen created a product-line of books (*Disrupting Class,*[5] *The*

Innovator's Prescription[6] and *The Innovative University*) and turned this idea into a mini consulting industry.

The third problem here is that Clay Christensen was a master salesperson (and engaging classroom teacher). Many people believed his theory about the importance of disruptive innovation without checking the history of the idea (e.g., Joseph Schumpeter theorised about the 'creative destruction' of businesses in 1942), the solidarity of the foundations on which this thesis was grounded (anecdotes) or the range of the theory (it is both a chronicle of the past [this has happened] and a model of the future [this will keep happening]).

As we noted earlier, academic and management consulting theories are often useful as a lens through which to generate and evaluate strategic options. However, they need to be understood before they are used. For example, two theories underpin the interest in e-learning technologies like MOOCs, and one questions the rate at which these courses are likely to be adopted. These theories are labour productivity, disruptive innovation and the adoption and diffusion of innovations.

Will MOOCs Be Disruptive?

In the 1960s, William Baumol and William Bowen described the situation where the salaries paid to people rise much faster than the productivity growth of these people.[7] In areas such as performing arts, nursing, public administration and education this situation is common. In higher education many functions require a similar amount of time to complete as they did 100 years ago, such as designing curriculum and examinations, marking a written essay, assessing a student special case, preparing a lecture, giving this lecture, running a tutorial, supervising a laboratory session. So MOOCs seem to offer a productivity breakthrough. By designing self-service into the course (such as self-paced content access, self-assessment and using social media technologies to get students to engage with each other) some functions can be streamlined, or at least pushed onto the students. Also, once designed and built, these courses are reusable without extra production costs and can be rolled out to vast numbers of students at the same time at minimal extra cost. Thus, the productivity of some aspects of a MOOC course can be increased dramatically.

Now consider the following prediction made in 2013 from two advocates of disruptive innovation that appeared in the Forbes Leadership Forum.

> A revolution is coming to U.S. higher education, one that will sweep away an archaic business model, erase the value of many venerable brands, and enhance the brands of new entrants and nimble incumbents. It will be a tough time for many U.S. colleges and universities but great news for the rest of the world.[8]

Does this dire prediction have any substance?

First, consider school education. The old technologies of books, classrooms and teachers have proved to be resilient to many new 'breakthrough' education technologies. Yes, classrooms are now more intelligent, but they are still recognisable as classrooms. And so are face-to-face lectures, tutorials, laboratory sessions and supervised examinations in universities. There is an intrinsic requirement about these old-style education technologies in the production of a 'university graduate'. And like schools, because a university has a social dimension and is an immersive experience, this requires context, such as human feedback from someone who knows more than the student, immersion time and guided learning.

Second, because MOOCs are an innovation, the theory of the adoption and diffusion of innovations is a useful guide to what is likely to happen. First, what is a MOOC? Richard Lyons, dean of the Hass School of Business at UC Berkeley, suggests that it is more a new distributional channel than a new educational product.[9] Hence, one benefit resides in receiving a course 'anytime, anywhere'. Subsidiary benefits include reduced travel time, the comfort of working in one's own space and sometimes freemium pricing—the ability to sample a course for free. There are costs, some of which relate to private and network information technology, some to the loss of face-to-face contact in a university environment (inspiration and networking) and some to the inferior learning outcomes that often occur. The learning outcomes may be enhanced when MOOCs evolve to be able to customise content to individual learning styles. So at present on the spectrum of innovations MOOCs sit more comfortably in the middle than the ends, namely as a 'step-change' rather than 'incremental' or 'radical' innovation. This suggests that their present disruptive capacity is more limited than the spruikers who are pushing them suggest.

Another reason for the slower than predicted adoption and diffusion of MOOCs is that they are trying to replace the dominant design of university education, much of which is built around face-to-face interaction, and, as we noted earlier, much of which involves living on campus. To illustrate how difficult some dominant designs are to break, consider that most readers of this book are using a QWERTY keyboard on their computer and phone. (It was originally designed to slow down typing speed, not to make it easy!) Also, innovation theory suggests that there will be a lot of trial and error before MOOCs either die or become a 'standard' product form. So, spare a thought for the President of the University of Virginia whose Board of Trustees tried to fire her in 2012 for failing to disruptively innovate with sufficient speed!

Third, it is not yet clear who MOOCs are aimed at. For example, most people who attend university want a certified credential. And most people who employ these graduates want to know that they have reached a reasonable standard of (examination tested) education. Hence, there is a well-developed market for the traditional university-style education, and it is not obvious how MOOCs will replace this time-honoured, immersive approach. So where might they gain traction?

One role for MOOCs is to offer courses for people who want to do small off-site units of university study that will count towards a degree (called micro-credentials). Another group is alumni who want convenient access to life-long or top-up learning. Another group is people who are curious about a topic rather than interested in a formal credential. Many retired people reside in this segment. Finally, there are people in countries with weak higher education systems and shortages of quality educators. Here, the lure of low-cost, high-quality, convenient education is great. If this segmentation persists, the different needs of each group will drive the design of different MOOCs.

So while some MOOCs are getting good numbers of attendees, at present many of these tend to be the fringe dwellers of a traditional university education. They are people who do not want to commit to a full degree or would not be admitted under the normal admissions criteria. Thus, MOOCs seem to be increasing the reach of the type of material universities produce rather than cannibalising the traditional student cohort. They seem to be more of a complement to a traditional university experience than a substitute for it.

Fourth, MOOCs are based on a different learning model to that offered by a university. So, if students really want to learn, then the current university model is far better than a MOOC. Some insights about learning from John Loughran, the dean of the faculty of education at Monash University, help to explain this argument.[10] In the past the model of much university education could be characterised as 'telling with teaching' and 'learning with listening'. YouTube and many MOOCs look a lot like this. However, today good educators use a much better model of learning to construct the university experience. They start with the objective of getting people to be knowledgeable of an area and capable of doing something with this knowledge. This requires—creating a need to know, developing ways to engage the student, drawing out the student's prior knowledge, developing a conceptual understanding of content, practising using the knowledge and building a trusting relationship and safe learning environment. This is best done in an environment with a big dose of face-to-face interaction, lots of reading, thinking, practising and talking with others about self-generated ideas.

Fifth, the spruikers of MOOCs suggest that these courses will be designed by the premier academics in each field. This is a contestable proposition because many of very best scholars do not to want to design and deliver this type of course. Their preference is to teach and work with postgraduates. So while these star professors might help design the content of some MOOCs, hopefully they will be developed and delivered by other people with suitable expertise.

Sixth, there is the tricky question of how much money a university can make from MOOCs. At least enough to cover development and operating costs, and then those associated with the inevitable stumbles that will occur as this educational technology develops. Then if these courses do become established, how will they be priced so as not to cannibalise the profitability of existing courses? The demand for curiosity and life-long learning is probably more price-sensitive and fickle than the demand for a certified degree from a traditional university that can be used to enter or progress through the workforce.

Our conclusion is that MOOCs and many other EdTech innovations are 'work in progress'. So from a strategic perspective, what might a well-established university do? Pankaj Ghemawat suggests that rather than ignore or switch over completely, one option is to straddle both the old and new technologies without many linkages between the two.[11] This at least signals that the university 'is doing something', whether this is true or not. Another option is to combine both technologies, for example by using MOOCs for fact-based learning and the more traditional methods for discursive learning, or using MOOCs as a part of the university entrance requirements, such as Harvard Business School's Credential of Readiness targeted at potential MBA students.

Another strategic question is how fast should a university move to embrace MOOCs? Like many others, we suggest that they become a 'fast follower' rather than 'disruptive innovator'. Fast followers learn from others' mistakes and can capitalise on the technological innovations of other players. Fast followers in this arena might use the services of groups like OES (Online Education Services), FutureLearn and 2U to help them develop material and navigate this new education space. Also, despite what journalists often report, being a fast follower is a less risky and a more likely route to success.

So since 2013, when the previous dire prediction was made, have these courses destroyed the dominant design of university teaching? Not yet. Have they disrupted the traditional university business model? Not yet. Have many of the early innovators failed? Yes. Are we surprised by the slower than expected impact of these courses on higher education? No. Will they eventually disrupt this long-established model? Probably not, but who knows. As we go to print the COVID-19 pandemic is forcing universities to shift most of their courses online. This exercise may boost the development of MOOCs or if the students think that it is delivering a weaker educational experience it may retard this development. Time will tell.

One potential disruption to the traditional education model of the 'standard' university could be developed in the world of gaming and social media. If the psychologists and neuroscientists who design the persuasive technologies that make interactive games and sites like Facebook and Snapchat so successful are asked to create new e-learning technologies, then they might disrupt the traditional forms of university teaching.[12]

5.5 Rankings: Managing to These Measures

An important strategic concern of many universities around the world is, how should they respond to the numerous rankings that purportedly measure their quality or more specifically their status? Remember the old saying that

> What gets measured, matters.

So, should a university play the status ranking game? And if they do, how should they play? Let's explore the second question first because universities do play the rankings game. Then we will suggest why this is the wrong game to play.

Playing the Ranking Game

During the era before these rankings were developed, academics looked inward and to each other for the attributes that defined quality, status and reputation. However, from a student point of view, many of these attributes, especially those related to research, were largely irrelevant to the quality of their education and whether this made them 'life-ready' or 'work-ready'. So some enterprising people and media outlets saw an opportunity to develop different measures of quality that were more transparent and useful to the people whose money was underwriting the university system. And without too much thought, the Australian government also bought into this idea. So what emerged was a system that reduced each university to a single number—its rank against its peers!

Simon Marginson and Mark Considine (*The Enterprise University*) suggest that many Australian universities now seek to advance their own prestige and status as an end in itself. In this game two compulsory rankings for Australia's universities are the Excellence in Research Australia (ERA) and the more recent Engagement and Impact (EI). The ERA is a government-imposed quality assurance system that grades selected areas of each university's research as above or below world standards. It has been run four times. Because it is now no longer used to directly allocate research funding, many universities view it as an expensive form of government red tape. One estimate was that the 2018 ranking cost close to $26 million to conduct.[13] However, it did suggest that 90% of the research submitted for evaluation was at or above world standard.[14] What it did not reveal was how much research was not presented for evaluation, and by implication, it's less than world-standard quality. The EI assessment reflects a significant change in thinking about the types of research the government values. There must now be a line-of-sight between research and its application or influence outside academic circles.

Three other rankings that are often used define the performance of Australia's major universities are the QS World University Ranking, the Times Higher Education World University Ranking and the Academic Ranking of World Universities (ARWU). While each one uses a different methodology, they all weight research as the most important attribute. For example, the QS World University Ranking measure is composed of the following items:

1. Academic reputation (40%)—based on a global survey of academics who are asked to identify the leading institutions in their field.
2. Employer reputation (10%)—based on a survey of graduate employers who are asked to identify the institutions producing the best graduates in their sector.
3. Student-to-faculty ratio (20%)—a commitment to high-quality teaching.
4. Research citations per faculty member (20%)—reflects the impact of research.
5. Proportion of international faculty (5%)—to reflect an institution's success in attracting faculty from overseas.
6. Proportion of international students (5%)—to reflect an institution's success in attracting students from overseas.

What is notable here is that notwithstanding the complexity of a modern university and its multiple aims, the underlying model is very simple and simplistic. The focus is clearly on academics, employers and surrogates for teaching. Nothing else matters—not equity, diversity, social inclusiveness, ethics, values, industry engagement or many of the other factors that populate the public statements of strategy. The other major reputation polls are equally focused. So any university that aspires for a strong social equity footprint is not doing this to help win the rankings game. It is doing this to create a separate citizenship reputation.

In general, rankings of the type in which universities seek to excel can be used for six purposes:

- As a signal of unobserved institutional quality, and thus
- as a decision aide for students, staff and donors.
- As an evaluation tool by the university's main bank and regulator—the government.
- As an evaluation tool of the vice chancellor by the university council.
- As a template for change—strategy and/or operations.
- As a vehicle to legitimise bragging rights for the best performers.

In their best light, rankings can motivate value-enhancing competition amongst universities. However, for this to occur they have to be good (valid and reliable) measures of quality. The academic community has conducted a large amount of research that looks at the scientific validity of these measures. Much of it is not very complementary.[15]

In their worst light, rankings can motivate value-decreasing operational decisions. For example, one way to game the rankings is to make sure that the university's reportable workforce (aka the academics who are counted in ranking scheme) are the active researchers. Now consider the following critique by the vice chancellor of one of Australia's best universities.

> Some universities are overtly manipulating their reportable workforce, converting, en masse, academics into teaching-only roles that break the link between higher education and research.
>
> Universities defend the segregation of the teaching and research workforces under the seemingly reasonable explanation of comparative advantage: let the best teachers focus on teaching, and let the best researchers focus on research. But in many cases, staff are tapped on the shoulder to take on large teaching loads not based on their teaching ability, but rather their perceived under-performance within research.

> And there are consequences. Many of the next generation of students will be taught entirely by people who are not creating new knowledge through research.
>
> Future students will ask, if I am not being taught by a research-active teacher, why exactly should I get my education at a university at all?
>
> Australian National University (ANU) Vice Chancellor Professor Brian Schmidt, 'A great university is first made by its students.' ANU website (7 November, 2019)[16]

From a strategic perspective the international rankings highlighted on a university's website identify the areas of research where the university should focus. They also indicate who might be considered as key competitors, namely, the other universities who also promote their place in the same ranking.

From a global perspective what these rankings reflect is a 'layering' of universities in terms of (mainly research) quality. As Peter Booth, a past deputy vice chancellor of the University of Technology Sydney, noted, in this layered market most of Australia's universities could be considered as 'middle-tier'.[17] He suggests that they will prosper only if they can identify and execute an appropriate strategy in this tier. In essence, he is suggesting that regardless of how hard they try, most of Australia's public universities will never become elite, global institutions.

A quick analysis of these rankings also uncovers a potential problem for Australia's universities. It is the rise of the Chinese universities, many of which now clearly outrank those in Australia. For example, an article in *The Economist* newspaper reported that in 2018 Tsinghua and Peking Universities are two of the best in the world.[18] And when it comes to scientific publications in the STEMM (science, technology, engineering, mathematics, medicine) disciplines, China has 6 universities in the top 15, while Australia has none. The problem here is that China is a source of a large number of international students. So the question arises that if the top Chinese universities have a better ranking than ours, why are the Chinese students coming to Australia? The answer will be a combination of factors such as education, emersion in a Western society, lifestyle and gaining points for resident status.

Playing the PR Game

A public relations problem for Australia's universities that play these rankings games is that when a person searches across the websites of a number of universities, the cherry-picking of rankings to brag about becomes very obvious and very annoying. This weakens any claim made by the university about its relative standing. It also weakens the perceived integrity and probity of the university. Surely model social citizens as our universities aspire to be would not engage in such blatant public relations hype!

Why Rankings Is the Wrong Game to Play

From a strategic perspective, seeking to better one's place in a status-ranking system is a competitor-focused strategy. It is a zero-sum game—for every winner there is a loser. To beat one's competitors requires understanding the rules of the game which are enshrined in each multi-attribute measure, and then doing better on most attributes. Some can be improved by the university's efforts, while some cannot. For example, if an international ranking has an attribute that focuses on graduate employment, then the economic conditions of the country largely determine graduate demand. And if the percentage of international students is important, then currency exchange rates are an important driver of performance here.

When the focus is on beating competitors, it is easy to become complacent about being customer-focused, especially when there is ambiguity about how the ranking metric actually drives customer satisfaction. For example, two of the factors in the QS World University Ranking are the proportion of international faculty and the research citations of the faculty. But how do these requirements make students more life-ready or work-ready? How do they increase student satisfaction with the educational experience?

To highlight the shortcomings of a competitor focus, consider the goal Morita-san (Akio Morita) set for Sony after World War II. He wanted the company to be known for quality. His bigger goal for Sony was to help make Japan known for quality. So Sony was playing a positive-sum game, because as its quality improved, so did Japan's quality, and with it the country's competitiveness. Quality is also a target that moves in the right direction because as it improves, customer expectations rise, and to meet these higher expectations, quality needs to improve further. Quality is much more customer-focused and value creating than beating a competitor.

Wouldn't it be nice if Australia's leading universities had the vision of Morita-san and set out to enhance quality and thus the reputation of Australia's universities rather than climb up various greasy ranking polls? We wonder if any Australian university will have the courage to formally disengage from the ranking game.

5.6 Strategic Reputation Management

Many universities confuse status and reputation. Status is one's position in a ranking such as those discussed earlier. In contrast, reputation is a broader evaluation of the university's citizenship and competence (in education and research).[19] So a university has at least three distinct reputations—one each for citizenship, education and research. Because each reputation will be driven by different sets of factors and be more or less relevant to different groups of stakeholders, and because they may or may not be correlated with each other, they need to be measured separately. In Australia some universities commission customised reputation surveys such as the one offered by the Reputation Institute, known as RepTrak™, in an attempt to unpack these reputations.

Reputation is important because it summarises a university's achievements—we have a world-class reputation for XYZ; it makes a promise about what to expect—we will uphold and enhance this reputation; and it acts as a performance bond to all the university's stakeholders—we will do nothing to damage this reputation. It is strategically important in a competitive market because a good reputation helps to attract students, staff, research funds and donations. It also helps to add gravitas and credibility to its communications and those of its staff. The reputation of a university is arguably its single most important intangible asset. Hence, you would expect that a statement of strategy would contain a clear set of investments and actions for building, maintaining and protecting reputation.

While the websites and published statements of strategy of many universities note their goal of doing well in various so-called reputation polls, there is seldom any direct mention of their three types of reputation. This is also the case in these institutions' annual reports. So one is left to assume that the implicit strategy is to engage more with industry and society (citizenship reputation), teach better (education reputation) and publish more (research reputation). But 'working harder' is not a corporate strategy or a reputation strategy.

5.7 Taking Stock

When we are asked to look at the strategy of an organization, we start by filling in the boxes in the following diagram. It is a bit like doing a stocktake. What does the organisation say are its objectives? What are its current capabilities? What are the key characteristics of the environment in which it competes for resources? Who are the target customers? The answers to these four simple questions should be clear in any strategy document. However, it is the links between them (the arrows in Fig. 5.1) that often reveal some nasty surprises.

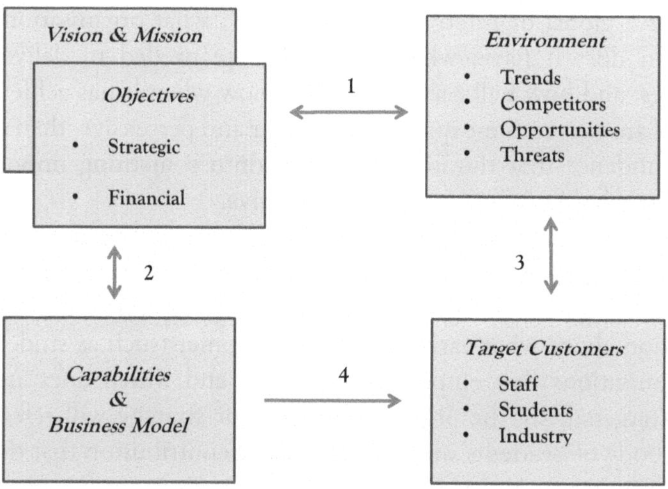

Fig. 5.1 Taking stock

Arrow #1 is a reality check. Sometimes this is called assessing external fit. Given what is happening in the external environment, are the organisation's objectives reasonable? A danger signal flashes when an organisation states its objectives without adequate reference to the conditions in the prevailing environment. This is one of our principal criticisms of Australia's public universities. They simply don't provide a clear snapshot of trends, opportunities, threats and competitors, or what will happen in the future. Hence, one can't determine the strength or weakness of Arrow #1.

Arrow #2 is another reality check. This is sometimes called assessing internal fit. Are the institution's capabilities and business model strong enough to meet its objectives? If a university states that it wants to make a global contribution in some form, then it will need some very strong capabilities. If it wants to become the number one teaching or research institution in Australia, then it needs to identify who currently holds this position and what capabilities will allow it to topple the incumbent. A danger signal flashes here when an organisation states an objective and it is not clear what capabilities or business model is needed to deliver it. For example, the Australian National University wants to be Australia's national university, and the University of New South Wales wants to be Australia's global university. But what is a national university, and what exactly is a global or international university; what organisational configuration does it have; what capabilities are needed to deliver these objectives, and how will each university know when it has achieved this status? If answers to these questions are clear and persuasive, then one can have confidence that the universities are onto something important—well, if stakeholders engage with the objective.

A key aspect of Arrow #3 is to calibrate the size and nature of demand for the university's products and services. That is, the opportunity to be successful. A good strategy will contain a precise and (data) informed description about what various types of customer (such as students and the organisations that employ them) want, and which ones are to be served (targeted) by the organisation. A poor strategy will refer to the general body of 'students' and 'industry'. The contribution that the discipline of marketing has made beyond that of economics is to model the heterogeneous nature and needs of stakeholders and students. For example, in the market for university ideas and services there are subgroups of students with different needs. Typically in statements of strategy universities use a very bland form of segmentation, namely, undergraduate and postgraduate; domestic and international; full-time and part-time. Such bland thinking obscures the needs and wants of the students and hampers developing innovative solutions to their needs. Because this is such an important issue, it deserves a bit more discussion.

There are more insightful segmentation schemes. For example, one is based on whether students are in a formative and developmental or practical and instrumental phase of their life. In the first group the experience of going (full time) to university is like time-released medicine. In the latter group it is like an energy supplement or pain-relief medicine. Another way that these segments can be formed is on the basis of students' views about where the value of their degree lies, such as in the programme (the years spent at university) or the knowledge (which helps to learn a living) or the letters of the degree (which helps to signal some special attributes of the student that will help him or her get a job at their preferred employer). Another way to segment students is by the type of courses they choose. Some have a fairly common global core of knowledge, such as business studies, computing, engineering and mathematics. Others have much local knowledge like teaching, nursing, political science, marine science, tourism and law. And then there is the group of students who go to the only university that offered them a place or the group that favours location and convenience over all other factors. These types of insights will help to understand the attributes of the university and its programmes that affect student choice. They will also suggest where the university should develop its capabilities. In marketing the procedure for doing this is called segmentation, targeting and positioning.[20]

So a good strategy statement will be clear and insightful about which types of students the university wants to attract, how many of these students might be attractive to the institution because it is positioned as a particular type of institution (such as a technology university or an educational university or a research-intensive university) and what types of employers recruit the graduates from various faculties. And for a university to make a major contribution to the workforce, which most of them state is a strategic priority, the nature of the derived demand for its graduates also needs to be understood. Questions like these need answers. Which (types of) organisations do and don't recruit from university? Do the same organisations recruit both full-time and part-time graduates?[21] Do organisations that recruit full-time graduates then put them through some internal training, or do they start work immediately? Where do overseas students get employed—if and when they go home? Answers to these questions hint at the strengths and weaknesses of University X.

Arrow #4 describes how the capabilities and business model of the organisation will deliver value to the targeted students and staff. It is the strategy of the organisation. A strategy only makes sense in the context of Objectives, Market, and Target Staff and Customers (students and employers). Without all three aspects of this context, the statement of strategy is ambiguous. As noted later, the strategy statements of Australia's public universities pen a lot of words on Mission and Objectives but far too few on the Market and Target Staff, Students and Employers. Hence, they are deficient as credible statements of strategy.

Figure 5.1 doesn't tell whether a strategy is good or not so good, but it does suggest some questions that a council member might ask the vice chancellor about what is proposed. In fact, the role of each framework discussed in this chapter is to provide a source of informed and informative questions about University X's strategy.

Notes

1. D. Siegel and S. Leih, "Strategic Management Theory and Universities: An Overview of the Special Issue", *Strategic Organization,* Vol. 16, No. 1 (2018), 6–11.
2. The academics did not mind this because it allowed them to accumulate teaching load in a short span of time and thus free up longer periods for research. Other academics were happy to be paid (at marginal cost to the university) for above-load teaching.
3. P. Nikoletatos, "Shaping sticky students: encouraging lifelong academic relationships in an era of transience", *Campus Review* (14 June, 2019).

4. For example, in 2007 Christensen told *Business Week* that Apple won't succeed with the iPhone. See A. A. King and B. Baatartogtokh, "How Useful Is the Theory of Disruptive Innovation?" *MIT Sloan Management Review*, Vol. 57, No. 1 (2015), 77–90 for somewhat thorough dismantling of the evidence used in Christensen's theory of disruptive innovation.
5. C. M. Christensen, M. B. Horn and C. W. Johnson, *Disrupting Class: How Disruptive Innovation Will Change the Way the World Learns* (New York: McGraw-Hill, 2011).
6. C. M. Christensen, J. H. Grossman and J. Hwang, *The Innovator's Prescription* (New York: McGraw-Hill, 2009).
7. W. J. Baumol and W. G. Bowen, *Performing Arts, The Economic Dilemma* (Cambridge, Mass.: MIT Press, 1966).
8. B. Guile and D. Teece, "The Real Winners of the Coming Revolution in Higher Education", *Forbes Leadership Forum* (12 March, 2013).
9. R. K. Lyons, Economics of the Ed Tech Revolution", *California Management Review*, Vol. 59, No. 4 (2017), 49–55.
10. J. Loughran, "Telling evidence on complexities of teaching", *The Australian* (12 September, 2018), p. 33.
11. P. Ghemawat, "Strategies for Higher Education in the Digital Age", *California Management Review*, Vol. 59, No. 4 (2017), 56–78.
12. See for example, H. Edwards, "The Masters of Mind Control", *Time* (23 April, 2018), 30–35.
13. T. Dodd, "ERA Winners but process Rankles", *The Age* (27 March, 2019).
14. This high number doesn't suggest that 90% of all a university's research is at or above world standard, only that the best research selected for evaluation is at this peer-reviewed level.
15. For example, T. Devinney, G. R. Dowling and N. Perm-Ajchariywong, "The Financial Times Business Schools Ranking: What Quality is this Signal of Quality?" *European Management Review*, Vol. 5 (2008), 195–208.
16. From http://www.anu.edu.au/news/all-news/a-great-university-is-first-made-by-its-students
17. P. Booth, "Middle-tier universities in Australia aren't doomed to wither and die", *The Conversation* (31 July, 2014).
18. "Looking to beat the world", *The Economist* (17 November, 2018), 33–34.
19. See for example, G. R. Dowling, *Winning the Reputation Game* (Cambridge: MIT Press, 2016).

20. G. L. Lilien and A. Rangaswamy, *Marketing Engineering* (DecisionPro, 2004).
21. For example, at the old Australian Graduate School of Management we found that the organisations that hired full-time MBA graduates were less likely to hire part-time EMBA graduates ($r = -0.7$).

6

What Are the Strategies of Australia's Universities? Environment, Competition, Resources and Capabilities

As noted in Chap. 3 the place to start thinking strategically is to review the environment in which a university operates. Here we focus on contemporary factors that pull universities in different directions and that challenge their evolutionary fitness. Information about the broad domain of higher education can be found on the Universities Australia website and in various reports such as *Mapping Australian Higher Education 2018* by the Grattan Institute[1] and *The University of the Future* by Ernst & Young.[2] It can also be found in books such as *University Governance and Reform*.[3] Tomes such as these dispel a common myth that Australian universities don't change very much. They chronicle how many changes are similar to those experienced by universities in other countries. For example:

- The nature of the resource markets has become more international with greater competition for students, academic staff and prestige
- The focus of universities has shifted from 'inside-out'—where they knew what was best, to 'outside-in'—where they now look for signals from government, society, the economy and overseas peer universities for what they should do

T. Devinney, G. Dowling, *The Strategies of Australia's Universities*,
https://doi.org/10.1007/978-981-15-3397-6_6

- Research has twisted itself into a system of measured performance rather than a process of curiosity-driven exploration, and within this regime academic performance has moved from 'publish or perish' to also include 'be cited or sidelined'
- Journal rating lists are replacing peer judgement as the best way to assess the quality of research
- Teaching must now respond to student (consumer) expectations in ways that were unthinkable in earlier times
- Universities are ruled more by centralised plans, formulas, targets, budgets and incentives, and money has become a meta-measure of success
- It is not clear where the responsibility for academic leadership and pastoral care now lie within the university
- The power of academic disciplines to shape agendas in universities is being replaced by cross-disciplinary or multi-disciplinary groups that are more susceptible to selection and influence from central administration
- Academic contracts have changed from 'you pretend to work and we will pretend to pay you' to performance-managed contracts
- Mid-level administrators now earn as much as many top-performing academics, and senior administrators earn more
- Universities are creating 'related entities' to help pursue market opportunities; some of these are outside the reach of traditional forms of university governance and collegial scrutiny
- Central administration now creates university-wide rules for teaching terms, grading, student evaluations of lecturers and courses, student appeals, composition of selection committees, academic promotion, ethics approval for research and so forth
- Central administration mediates many of the interactions between the university and its external constituencies
- Federal government policy has become a system of limited funding and discretionary payments
- Competition with other universities for fee-paying students and research grants has increased
- Operational performance is often directed by the requirements of government oversight agencies

- Many university activities are designed to fit the requirements of outside accreditation institutions and their publication of league tables
- The adoption of standard human resource practices such as performance development and appraisal schemes has shed a light on the previous secret life of the academic
- The NPM regime of university governance and management has strengthened the role of the management executive relative to the academics
- Few vice chancellors have the track record to be seen as academic leaders
- The increased necessity to lure international fee-paying students
- The implementation of full-cost and market-based tuition fees
- The increasing use of casual labour, namely, postdoctoral students and casual teachers
- Research is becoming more of a cost-recovery activity, and education a source of revenue
- Growth in the size of most universities
- A greater reliance on information technology in every facet of university life
- The poaching of star academics from one university to another such that universities have become 'holding companies' for mobile, entrepreneurial researchers
- The evolution of many universities from elite (research) institutions to educational finishing schools.

This list suggests that our universities have experienced some profound changes over the last few decades. The environment in which they operate will generate more such change.

Every strategy consulting firm and every strategy textbook have their own template to guide gathering and organising information about the environment in which an organisation operates. We call this analysis the backstory of strategy. Our aim in this chapter is not to identify every factor that may influence how universities will survive and prosper, but rather to outline the types of information that need to be analysed to create the context for strategy. As noted earlier, without this context it is impossible to gauge the feasibility of a university's strategy. A context-light statement of strategy is really just a fictional story; it lacks credibility.

6.1 The Strategy Backstory

Describing the external environment of a university needs a framework to guide the collection and integration of information. A common framework is PEEST which refers to political, economic, environmental, social and technology environments. To this we add two Cs for customers and competition. Following a brief description of these aspects of the external environment, we will illustrate how a university could assess the strength of its resources and capabilities—its internal environment.

The External Environment: PEEST + C + C

Somewhere in the central administration of the university should reside a lengthy document that contains the following types of information. For example:

- *Political*—How federal government regulations, funding formulas and visa requirements for overseas students influence the revenue and costs of the university.
- *Economic*—How changing macro-economic conditions affect the capacity for governments to underwrite university funding. How changing industry structures and workforce demands influence the demand for university graduates and research.
- *Environmental*—How changes in the natural environment create a new set of problems and issues for society, and how these influence the operations of the university and its education and research agendas.
- *Social*—How demographic and social changes influence the expectations about a modern university. How trends like the democratisation of knowledge and the development of a global knowledge society will impact on a university's role in civil society.
- *Technology*—How technology helps to deliver the desired student experience and might disrupt this in the near future.
- *Competition*—The nature of competition from other Australian and overseas universities for students and academics and how this impacts the costs, revenue and reputation of the university.

- *Customers aka Students*—What the demands of different segments of students place on the university and how a greater fee-for-service regime will change the nature of their university education and their relationship with the institution.

Universities will summarise and interpret this information in different ways. For example, some recent research has indicated that many undergraduate students now act more like 'customers' than 'students'.[4] They are not afraid to move to another institution if they feel dissatisfied, unfulfilled or disengaged. They would also attend multiple universities at one time if subjects could be consolidated and credited towards one degree. Loyalty to an institution is becoming secondary to value for money from the 'product' of education—the degree. In this circumstance a strategic goal of being the institution for the life-long learning of its undergraduates becomes problematic. These students will shop around for postgraduate, mid-career and passion project education. This is what we referred to earlier as the weak spot at the bottom of a university. If as Professor Brian Schmidt says, a great university is first made by its students, then the changing nature of this group and their relationship with the institution are critical. As we note later, many universities are sending contradictory signals about what they want this relationship to be.

Some universities form the information above into a model of the higher education system and their place in it. Others will create scenarios of the future. Notwithstanding the approach taken, what matters is to identify trends (such as the demand for university education), interactions (such as how changes in government policy trigger other changes in the higher education sector), dependencies (such as the extent to which the sustainability of one's university depends on, say, the government funding, student demand or various sources of external funding), risks (such as students acting more like customers) and sector-wide threats and opportunities (e.g., that might be triggered by advances in information technology). Most statements of strategy make passing reference to a number of the PEEST + C + C factors, but few provide a comprehensive picture of either the current situation or what the future might hold. As noted next, this has enticed some consulting companies to produce sector-wide analyses.

6.2 The University of the Future

A report by the consultants Ernst & Young recently did the rounds of many of Australia's universities.[5] It is one of those snapshots of the future type of consulting briefs. It was titled *The University of the Future* and provides an illustration of the background strategy information discussed above. It used the technique of scenario analysis. Based on their review of the university sector, which included interviews with university leaders, employers and students, the consultants describe four different types of university of the future. Here are brief descriptions:

- Champion University—which is the government-funded university of today, but with more streamlined operations and administration.
- Commercial University—a more financially independent university with much closer ties to industry.
- Disruptor University—the government deregulates the sector to drive diversity, competition and efficiency; universities leverage the new information dissemination technologies; they expand into new educational markets with new services.
- Virtual University—the government restructures the tertiary sector to integrate universities and vocational institutes, prioritising training and employability outcomes.

A key strategic issue that emerged from the interviews with university leaders was that they were aware of the tension between optimising their current business model (the Champion University idea) and investing in the technologies that might lead to future disruption (the Disruptor and Virtual Universities). In strategy parlance this is often referred to as 'running today' and 'building tomorrow'. So in a strategy statement we would expect to see clear plans for both sets of activities. Also, there needs to be a clear line-of-sight between running today and the intended university of tomorrow. But this begs the question of 'what will tomorrow look like?'

As you might expect, Ernst & Young makes some predictions and recommendations. It predicts that the Commercial and Disruptor Universities are most likely to emerge. They will out-compete the incumbents. They also suggest that creating these new universities will require shifting from being faculty-focused to learner-centric, collaborating with industry to co-create educational material, integrating with industry to facilitate knowledge transfer, reimagining the physical campus for the digital world and unbundling degree programmes and the university value chain. If a university followed this recipe, it would not look much like its current form.

What is notable about these scenario summaries and their more detailed discussion in the report is that one of the sustainable competitive advantages of universities is missing, namely, research. It has become a background issue rather than a foundation aspect of a modern university in a knowledge-based economy. Because the research role of universities is so critical to the future prosperity of Australia, a research-led university must also be worth considering. Hence, we could also envisage this university of the future:

- R&D University—a research and development-focused university organised around clusters of complementary disciplines (like biopharmaceutical and medical engineering sciences) that produce research-led education (of medical professionals), and leverages its intellectual capital into innovations (new medical procedures) and human services (like a university hospital).

What is also notable about the Ernst & Young think piece is that it ignores the fact of student diversity, or segmentation as we called it in the previous chapter. And because of this it ignores some obvious opportunities for universities. For example, the University of Phoenix in the USA is designed to serve a specific type of student with a specific type of need, namely, working adults and military personnel who need to upskill or re-enter the workforce after a protracted break. They offer professional development short courses, certificate programmes, recertification programmes and degrees. The programmes are delivered online or on one of two campuses. Another example is from China. It is a university for the elderly. For example, at Shanghai University for the Elderly the average age of students is 65–70. This idea began in France in 1973 as the University of the Third Age movement, named for the last third of one's life. As Australia ages and self-funded retirees seek life after work, there could be a big opportunity to provide a traditional university-style education for ex-professionals to pursue new intellectual challenges.

While reports like the one produced by Ernst & Young are useful inputs to strategy, each university must make its own analysis because these exercises need to be anchored against the current resources and capabilities of the university. In other words, given that the future of a university depends on its past, how feasible would any of these chosen visions be? And are other universities likely to crowd out some opportunities? Because we have been critical of an almost total lack of discussion about competition in most of the current statements of strategy, this topic needs some further discussion.

6.3 Competition and Rivalry

Competition and rivalry is a central aspect of strategy. First, universities compete with a range of outside beliefs and organisatons. For example, there are many students who would be welcomed by a university but who believe that these institutions are 'not worth the money'. There are many academically inclined people who can earn better remuneration outside the university sector. There are many professional associations like Engineers Australia that offer training for new graduates and professional development programmes for members. And nearly all major corporations offer in-house training programmes that compete with university education.

In the Australian university sector the basic rules of competition are shaped by the commonwealth government—its funding model, data requirements and quality assurance agencies. So universities are encouraged to compete with each other, but they are funded and measured on common metrics. One outcome of these parameters of competition is that they discourage radical institutional innovation. In this circumscribed world Marginson and Considine note that the winning formula is to combine status advantage with institutional coherence and a broad-based, vibrant scholarly culture.[6]

Rivalry occurs between members of the same segment of universities, such as the Sandstone universities competing for the top Australian position on a particular ranking. Rivalry also occurs between segments, such as the Sandstone and the Redbrick universities who compete with the Sandstone universities in the cities in which both are located. Rivals are often called a strategic group. For example, it is unlikely that the actions of James Cook University will affect the Australian National University. However, the actions of the University of Sydney (Sandstone) and the University of New South Wales (Redbrick), both members of the Group of Eight (Go8) research universities located in Sydney, will affect each other. For example, when UNSW established its Scientia Professorships, it may have drawn some star professors away from the University of Sydney. Also, both these Go8 universities compete for the best and brightest Sydney-based school students. They also compete for donations from the local Sydney community.

Another aspect of competition is between the image of the old and the new. For example, the Gumtree and Unitech universities like to try to distance themselves from old-fashioned notions of academia and present a persona of innovation and the development of new fields of study such as communications, artificial intelligence and the recently fashionable 'big data'. Another way that the universities compete with each other is to make sure they have a medial and/or biological sciences faculty. If not, then pharmacy, dentistry, veterinary or nursing will suffice. These faculties immediately confer prestige on the institution. Also, these are the faculties that have access to the largest amounts of external research funding.

What is interesting about competition and rivalry is that there is seldom any mention in a university's strategy statement about how it will compete in its resource markets or in the rankings for prestige and status. Most universities are also silent about the primary catchment area for their students—local, state, national or international. And unlike the commercial sector where it is common for employees to know their direct competitors, there is seldom a conversation in Australia's public universities about who competes with whom. It is as though each university can do as it wishes without the fear of triggering any reaction from other universities, even those within sight of each other.

Managers typically bring a distinctive mindset to competition. Some set out to beat their competitors, while others set out to avoid competitors. The beat-competitor strategies are often a version of—be more innovative, spend more money or work harder, smarter and faster. In a university context such a strategy would be implemented by outspending competitors on infrastructure and marketing, and setting higher targets for teaching and research. In contrast to this approach, some organisations like to develop strategies that allow them to avoid direct competition and the short-term profit destroying outcomes that often result. Targeting specific segments of students, like the University of Phoenix case earlier, is one such example.

The strategy literature has many frameworks to help identify competitors and gauge their potential to disrupt a university's best-planned strategy. Some like Michael Porter's Five Forces model focus on industry competition.[7] Others like game theory and the payoff matrix focus on the moves and countermoves of two or more competitors in a particular market. Notwithstanding which frameworks are chosen to model competition, the first step for a university is to specify:

- Which universities are its rivals
- What impact does the actions of the university have on these rivals
- How rivals will react to these actions
- How the university will react to the actions of its rivals
- Are there any rules that govern how institutions react to each other

Because the last requirement may not be intuitive, consider the case of the Australian retail banks. The rules for interest rate changes are clear and generally followed. Each of the big banks takes its turn in being the first to change interest rates, and the others dutifully follow in a short period of time. They also signal to each other via media releases that an interest rate change is likely. Thus, there are few surprises, and the chance of one bank overreacting to another bank's interest rate move is lessened. The idea here is for the banks to avoid competition where it might really hurt their profits. Competition is assigned to other arenas such as customer service. This is one reason why Australia's Big Four retail banks are some of the most profitable in the world.

Another key aspect of strategic rivalry in the university sector is whether and how rivals might cooperate. For example, most of the Sydney-based universities have a programme to educate indigenous Australians. All struggle for numbers. So wouldn't it make sense to pool resources and aggregate students to form one good-quality programme? As we write this section the University Technology Sydney has just announced a $100-million, 250-bed residential college for indigenous students. The college will be built within walking distance of both the UTS and University of Sydney campuses. Surely the joint use of this facility would benefit both universities. There are many other areas where rivalry could be replaced by cooperation, such as the training of doctoral students.

6.4 The Internal Environment: Resources and Capabilities

Each university has its own unique portfolio of resources—human, location, infrastructure, organisational culture, reputation and endowment. It also has two sets of capabilities that allow it to do certain things, some better than others. One set is operational in nature and drives organisational efficiency such as the university's information technology, human resource and budget management systems. These are usually the responsibility of a chief operating officer and the chief financial officer. The other set of capabilities is dynamic in nature and the responsibility of the vice chancellor. These are the institution's ability to sense and seize opportunities and avoid threats and reconfigure organisational processes to exploit these factors. Dynamic capabilities, as they are called, underpin the evolutionary fitness of the university. They also help the institution respond to the opportunities and threats identified in the PEEST + C + C analysis outlined earlier. Hence, a good description of these is necessary.

After the 2018 Federal Government Engagement and Impact Assessment report, many universities decided they needed to better communicate their externally focused internal capabilities. What is notable about these efforts is that many capability statements confused the desire to do something and some current activity with an actual capability. The capability statements talked more about surface indicators than any differentiating capability. For example, the University of Wollongong statement listed 24 capabilities, ranging from being 'committed to pursuing a transformative agenda' in improving the health of older people to having 'an international reputation for the strength of our biomedical research and capability to develop biomaterial devices'. No concrete evidence supported any claim.

Universities have two core capabilities, namely, their research and their pedagogy. The type of painstaking research carried out by universities gives them a competitive advantage over all but the largest research laboratories and innovative companies in the world. And the type of immersive education combined with the award of a recognised degree gives universities a competitive advantage over other types of post-school education. These are the capabilities that provide the engagement opportunities found in the capability statements of the University of Wollongong and its peers. Just because a university has a degree programme or a research centre doesn't mean it has a recognised capability. All it suggests is that it has an interest in the area. Capabilities take massive investment and time to build a strong track record of achievement.

What is also characteristic of many capability statements is the siloed nature of the institution's resources and capabilities. Seldom do capabilities cross-pollinate each other like research-informed teaching. And seldom is there any discussion of how specific capabilities will be brought to bear to engage particular aspects of the institution's (hostile, benign or attractive) environment.

The strategic challenge for universities is to identify their key resources and operational and dynamic capabilities, then determine how these will be used to underpin their strategy and if and when some of these will need upgrading or replacing. To illustrate some of the strategic issues at play here, consider how the following two key resources of a university help implement its strategy.

Infrastructure

One of the first things noticed when visiting any Australian university is its location and campus. For example, the old sandstone campus of the University of Adelaide is simply stunning. It signals history, success, privilege and gravitas. For many staff and students, it adds to the experience of 'going to university'. Its location in the city signals that the university is a special place. Similarly, many of the modern buildings of the University of Technology Sydney, located as they are in a vibrant part of Sydney, signal youth and vitality. They help to add to the experience of going to this metropolitan university. Many academics criticise their vice chancellors for investing in bricks and mortar (rather than salaries), but a nice campus is like a nice house, something to look forward to going to. In the early years when we were at the University of New South Wales the 'redbrick' campus was very unappealing. It was so bad that it actually put some students off going to the university.

Recall how The Australian National University wants to entice more students to live on campus so they can experience a richer university life. Many other universities have a similar goal. They understand that their campus is a tangible strategic asset. The campus precinct is the hub that enriches academic and student life. It becomes a sacred site—think here of Harvard, Oxford and Cambridge. However, our universities then do two things that negate some of the usefulness of this asset. The first is to design some of the most boring academic office accommodation imaginable. This and the difficulty in getting a parking space (at a city campus) motivate many academics to spend more time in their home office than in their university office. So here we see a key aspect of staff-student interaction being designed out of the campus experience. The second thing is to encourage academics to put their lectures and other course material on the Internet so that the students can access them at their convenience. What now happens is that class attendance drops dramatically. Key buildings are underutilised, and the opportunity for student-student and student-teacher interaction is diminished.

People

Because academic staff is a key resource, a strategy should be clear about how this group is attained and retained. The University of New South Wales strategy is one of the few that went beyond banal statements of equity and diversity, encouraging excellence and people matter. It has established a 'unique Scientia approach to research and teaching excellence'.[8] This is explained in various parts of its strategy document as recruiting the best academics, offering them distinctive career pathways and supporting them to deliver excellence. Because academics love titles, giving this one a Latin name adds just a little bit more cachet to the position. Becoming a Scientia Professor is a sought-after appointment. From a strategic perspective, if UNSW can learn how to further strengthen and leverage these professorships, this will become a key part of the university's core capabilities. It will become an important point-of-difference. And it will help attract external stars and keep internal stars.

All universities are trying to develop their capabilities in the area of recruiting the best and brightest students—because quality here generally produces quality graduates. Also, there are significant investments in teaching and student learning centres as well as information technology that can help curriculum development and the learning experience. These are often mentioned in the statements of strategy. However, what is seldom mentioned is the tension that (growth) targets for student enrolments put on student quality. There have been a number of cases where entry standards have been lowered to the point where the media proclaim that some of our universities are in a race to the bottom of the student pool. It is a brave strategy that builds in transparent protocols that avoid compromising student entry standards. And a doubly brave strategy to also have protocols to uphold assessment standards. As many front-line teaching academics will attest, it is hard to fail a full-fee-paying student, even if they have never been seen in the classroom.

6.5 Organisational Culture

Finally, a key intangible resource of a university that can only be seen through the eyes of its staff and students is the culture of the university. Organisational culture is the system of shared values (what is important) and beliefs (how things work) that interact with the organisation's people, structures and protocols to produce behavioural norms (the way we do things around here).[9] It is an invisible web that binds the people in the university together. It also translates the values of the university into staff and student behaviour.

A concern expressed by many academics is the tension between two broad types of university culture—that of the college (or clan) and the corporation. The drivers of this tension are issues such as focusing teaching on critical education versus vocational training, focusing research on the public good versus industry concerns, the universities being more entrepreneurial and universities growing by increasing the size of the international student cohort. There is confusion about whether or how both cultures can peacefully coexist. And even within the college culture, there is a tension between whether research or teaching should define the institution. Organisational culture is a powerful force in strategy formation and implementation.

Regardless of the blend of cultures, the strategic issue is how to motivate the desired mix of excellence. Promotion criteria send a clear signal to the academics, as do work contracts. For example, the old standard contract was 40/40/20 whereby 40% of a person's time was devoted each to teaching and research and 20% to administration and engagement. This promoted the development of an 'all round' academic. It reflected the fact that universities were the only place where its key employees did both teaching and research. It also meant that many academics were interchangeable. When somebody was on leave or left the institution, it was easy to find a replacement from within the group.

Today, many universities are moving away from the widespread use of blended contracts. As noted by the ANU vice chancellor earlier, more and more academic staff are being forced into more unbalanced contracts where most of their load is devoted to teaching or research. The philosophy behind these contracts can be described using the language of strategy—the comparative advantage of letting people focus on what they are best at. It can also be described using the language of performance management—pay people (well) for what they do well, and don't pay people for what they can't do, or what they don't want to do.

An extreme version of this approach is being implemented by some Chinese universities that highly reward academics for research excellence. Here, money and tenure are the levers. As *The Economist* article mentioned earlier notes, the government funding system motivates universities to produce top-class research. Then the universities give their academics a direct monetary incentive to publish in a set of recognised journals. For example, bonuses can reach up to 20 times the salary of the average academic for a publication in *Nature*. This research focus is supported by an army of PhD students. Next, some Chinese universities have adopted a US-style tenure system—six years of research and teaching, then a performance review at which the academic is hired permanently or asked to leave. This creates a tough, uncompromising culture.

The new Chinese system is designed to play the short-term research rankings game, but it is not designed to win the 'big breakthrough' research game, and hopefully a Nobel Prize as the Chinese lust for. Because many big breakthroughs involve long-term concerted effort, some unorthodox thinking and often cross-disciplinary collaboration, this is not a game for the faint-hearted. So a research strategy needs to be careful about what it actually rewards. If tenure, promotion and significant salary bonuses come from publishing many bite-sized research papers that are designed for a specific set of journals, then this is most likely what the profile of the university's research will look like. Also, if the current generation of PhD students are trained in this environment, then expect most of them to play this game when they graduate.

To a large extent many of Australia's public universities are playing a similar game to their Chinese counterparts. When the Excellence in Research Australia (ERA) scheme was introduced, it established sets of quality indexed journals that have been only slightly modified over the years. Many of these lists have worked their way into the academic performance appraisal criteria of the universities. For example, in some schemes, these journals are awarded points based on their quality ranking. Then an academic is expected to publish papers that accumulate a required number of points in order to be evaluated as research active and publishing at a deemed level of quality. Typically more senior academics are expected to generate a greater number of points. Over time the way to increase research performance is to increase the number of points required.

For many junior academics this type of scheme motivates performance. However, for senior academics, it often diverts effort away from tackling risky research projects of the type that will make significant breakthroughs. You don't tend to get Nobel Prize–quality research by setting points-based research goals. This type of scheme trivialises the motivation for doing good research. Also, as James Wilson's report to the UK government suggests, the over-reliance on hard metrics and algorithmic systems of performance restricts research diversity and inadequately reflects its social impact.[10] The Institute for Advanced Study at Princeton, described earlier, was set up to deliberately avoid such stupidity.

A faculty with a strong research culture knows which people are research active, and what research is having impact without having to count papers. Maybe we should consider one of Albert Einstein's insights about counting things.

> Not everything that can be counted counts, and not everything that counts can be counted.

6.6 Strategic Fit

Strategy consultants typically have a framework to profile the opportunities and threats facing an organisation and how its resources and capabilities might be used to exploit this environment. The worst such framework is SWOT. Internal factors are sorted into Strengths and Weaknesses, while those in the external environment are sorted into Opportunities and Threats. The big weakness of this approach is that it produces four laundry lists of factors—the organisation's strengths and weaknesses, and the environment's opportunities and threats. A second weakness is that assessing each group of factors is left largely to the whim of the people creating the lists. For example, is government funding a strength or weakness? It is both because it underwrites a large part of the base funding of the university, but it is not enough. A third weakness of SWOT and other list-based approaches is that they ignore the interactions amongst factors. That is, a strength or weakness is contingent on a specific opportunity or threat. It is also contingent on the strengths and weaknesses of the organisation's rivals. For example, developing a good university research office is only strategically useful if it helps to win more external research grants than competitors, which again is contingent on the research done by the university needing the current sources of external research funding. In combination, these shortcomings mean that SWOT really stands for a Substantial Waste Of Time.

Figure 6.1 offers an alternative to SWOT. It describes an audit process built on the logic of—given a vision to become a certain type of university, look at the points where the university and key parts of its external environment intersect. To keep things simple, Fig. 6.1 profiles just three programmes—teaching, research and industry engagement. The idea is to ask a question at each point of intersection. These questions focus on capabilities, competitive advantage and the value proposition offered to students. For example:

1. Does the university have the capability to design and offer education that produces 'in-demand graduates'?
2. Does the university have the capability to do world-class research in the STEM sciences?
3. Does the university have the capability to work effectively with local industry?
4. How does teaching compare to competitors in our strategic group?
5. How does our research rank against our peers and competitors?
6. How strong are our industry partnerships relative to our competitors?

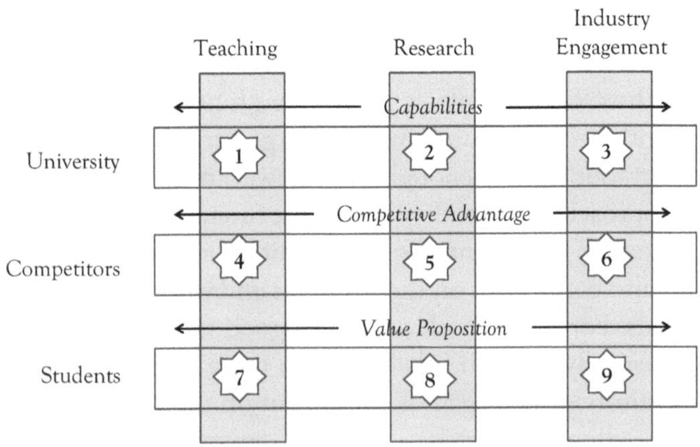

Fig. 6.1 Nine audit questions

7. What do students think of our curriculum, teaching and overall education?
8. How attractive to students are our research capabilities and outputs?
9. How attractive to students are our industry partners?

Questions 1, 2 and 3 focus on the capabilities of the university to achieve its stated objectives. For example, the University of New South Wales aspires to produce 'in-demand graduates', do world-class research and be the preferred partner for specific types of industry engagement. Looking at the institution's programmes to deliver these outcomes and measures of success (such as graduate employment, research rankings and industry preference) will reveal the strengths and weaknesses of its resources and capabilities.

Questions 4, 5 and 6 focus on competitive advantage. Here the first task is to identify the institution's (international) peers and competitors. At present, modesty or embarrassment seems to preclude this information from appearing in the public statements of strategy of our universities. It would be interesting to see a clear statement of how University X seeks to beat University Y for inputs (such as students, academics, funding and industry partners) and outputs (such as quality graduates, research and industry innovation) across specific arenas of operation.

Questions 7, 8 and 9 focus on the value propositions offered to students across teaching, research and industry engagement. For example, what do students think of the education model—old-style face-to-face or blended or new-age MOOC? Does current research really inform course material—do the professors teach, or do the part-time staff run the courses? Will students get the chance to hear from and/or engage with industry partners? And so the list goes on. Most statements of strategy make vague promises about some of these important issues. For example, the University of Newcastle says that 'our outstanding staff inspire and support students. The UON student experience prepares our graduates to be global citizens, leaders and entrepreneurs who are eager for life's challenges and will change their world for the better'. This sounds like cheerleading or advertising 'puffery'.

Mapping a university's strategic capabilities against its environment asks the simple question—'Can we achieve our objectives with our current resources and capabilities?' If the answer is no, the institution has to invest more in its resources and capabilities or revise its goals.

In the next two chapters we look at vision (Chap. 7) and objectives (Chap. 8). Here we see that vision is often derived from a vague notion of a particular type of university of the future, such as being a 'global university' or a 'national university' or a 'technology university' or a 'third age university' or a 'virtual university'. And what is troubling is that often a university's objectives will be divorced from, or tangential to, its vision. So when faced with a vague vision and scattered set of objectives, it is little wonder that other aspects of strategy are confused or ambiguous.

Notes

1. A. Norton, I. Cherastidthan and W. Mackey, "Mapping Australian higher education 2018", Grattan Institute (Carlton, VIC: September, 2018).
2. R. Cawood, et al., *The University of the Future* (EY Australia, 2018).
3. H. Schuetze, H. Bruneau and W. Grosjean (Eds), *University Governance and Reform: Policy, Fads and Experience in International Perspective* (Palgrave Macmillan US, 2012). See also, M. Shattock, "University governance in flux. The impact of external and internal pressures on the distribution of authority within British Universities: a synoptic view", working Paper no. 13, *Higher Education Funding Council for England* (February, 2017).
4. P. Nikoletatos, "What does a superior educational experience look like from the student perspective?" *Campus Review* (23 August, 2019).
5. R. Cawood, et al., *The University of the Future* (EY Australia, 2018).
6. S. Marginson and M. Considine, *The Enterprise University: Power, Governance and Re-invention in Australian Higher Education* (Cambridge, UK: Cambridge University Press, 2000).
7. M. Porter, *Competitive Strategy* (New York: Free Press, 1980).
8. Scientia is Latin for knowledge (science, skill, expertness).
9. From B. Uttal, "The Corporate Culture Vultures" *Fortune,* (17 October, 1983), 66–72.
10. J. Wilson, et al., *The Metric Tide: Report of the Independent Review of the Role of Metrics in Research Assessment and Management* (UK Government, DOI: 10.13140/RG.2.1.4929.1363, 2015).

7

What Are the Strategies of Australia's Universities? Mission, Vision and Values

Mission, vision and shared values are the soul of the university. Many people sign on for a university experience because its mission resonates with one or more of their fundamental beliefs. For example, at his speech to the World Academic Summit in 2018 Brian Schmidt, the vice chancellor of the Australian National University suggested that a fundamental role of universities is to increase the stock of knowledge available to the world so that this can be used to help design and implement pathways to a prosperous and sustainable global future.[1] He went on to argue that this knowledge should not be subject to justification by its direct utility to society, especially after being filtered by the current political mood. 'The unfiltered pursuit of knowledge is the building block of all that we do.' Many research academics would wholeheartedly support this mission, and a university that vigorously upheld its key principles.

The values of a university are designed to guide its mission. Each university lists a number of these either in their statement of strategy or on their website. For example, at the time of writing the University of Technology's values were discover, engage, empower, deliver and sustain. For the University of Western Australia these were respect, passion, excellence, integrity and diversity. For the University of Tasmania they were

T. Devinney, G. Dowling, *The Strategies of Australia's Universities*,
https://doi.org/10.1007/978-981-15-3397-6_7

honesty, integrity, responsibility, trust and trustworthiness, respect and self-respect, and fairness and justice that act as the basis for collective principled action. Most such value lists are generic and only tangentially speak to the fundamental purpose of the university. Many organisations could happily adopt them.

What is also interesting about such lists of values is what is missing. For example, if academic reputation is a key goal of a university, we would expect to see some values that speak directly to establishing and maintaining such a reputation, such as academic freedom and scientific professionalism. Also, it is rare to find any discussion of transparency. Transparency is important because this value underpins being open about the identity of donors and research partnerships and supplying evidence to support some key statements of fact found in strategy narratives. For example, a recurring issue is the claim that entry standards into some undergraduate degrees are falling. However, seldom is this key reputation issue addressed with data.

Sometimes part of the soul of the university might appear in its motto or its mantra. From a creative perspective some statements catch the eye. For example, the values of the University of South Australia play on the word 'ideas', which is something that universities are supposed to generate. They are integrity and accountability; diversity and social justice; engagement and collaboration; agility and innovation, and scholarship and excellence. For other universities it takes a bit of detective work to figure out their mission. For example, the University of New South Wales' (UNSW) motto is 'Scientica Manu et Mente'—'Knowledge by Hand and Mind'.

Both these approaches to communicating mission are 'usefully vague' so that a person can read into them as much or as little relevance as they desire. They are also hard to criticise. So their strength is also their weakness. They are just 'words', which are unlikely to offend but also unlikely to have much impact on the day-to-day lives of the members of the university.

Often the mission, vision or values of the institution are used to introduce its statement of strategy. For example, in its *2015–2020 Strategic Plan: Growing Esteem* the University of Melbourne states that it 'remains committed to being one of the finest universities in the world, contributing to society in ways that enrich and transform lives'. University of New South Wales wants to be 'Australia's global university'. The University of Newcastle wants to be 'a global leader in its commitment to equity and excellence and to create a better future for its regions'. The Australian National University wants to be 'the national university'. The University of Western Australia wants 'to provide world-class education, research and community engagement for the advancement of the prosperity and welfare of our communities'. In essence, these universities are telling a new-style Greek tragedy as expressed in the old motto of the Leo Burnett advertising agency, namely, that 'when you reach for the Stars, you might not quite get one, but you won't come up with a handful of mud either'.

You can't argue with these lofty aspirations—and that's the problem with them! They are warm and fuzzy and inoffensive. They are so generic and grand that they are really out of reach for most people. Many are also interchangeable amongst our universities. So where do these statements come from?

Grand visions and their accompanying lists of values tend to be made up by the university vice chancellor and the council. Sometimes this is informed by focus group discussions involving mixed groups from within the university. These discussions are often seeded by reading what other august universities around the world aspire to be. The two constraints that a vision statement faces are to make sure that it is different to that of other universities (to avoid blatant plagiarism), and inclusive so that it does not antagonise any particular group of stakeholders. They are designed to be grand statements of current best practice. However, more often than not, they wind up mimicking those of their peers.

For vision and values to be strategic they have to motivate people to deliver the university's aspirations and abide by its internal code of conduct. The best way to achieve this is to make sure that there is a 'direct line-of-sight' between institutional values, work processes and the key performance indicators (KPIs) of staff. Otherwise they are easily ignored. For example, two of the values of the University of Western Australia are the achievement of aboriginal peoples' aspirations and sustainability in the environment. But how many staff members have a specific KPI that reflects these values? And how would the university know when it has successfully achieved these outcomes?

Having a vague and sometimes vacuous mission and vision is not a problem that is unique to universities. Here is a test for the reader—can you state the mission and values of the organisation in which you work? Can you state its motto? We recently did a study of this type of recall and found that very few employees can.

Notwithstanding the unlikely day-today use of these statements, universities do need some overarching strategic purpose to help them define their place in the world and answer the key strategic question: 'What is the fundamental purpose, end or goal of an Australian public university?'

7.1 The Theory of a University and Its Telos[2]

A university needs a coherent and morally grounded theory of what it is.[3] For example, is it an institution that makes people 'life-ready' or does it seek to make them 'work-ready' or does it seek to create 'a better society'? A life-ready institution could be a community of students and scholars that creates and disseminates knowledge to advance society and its citizens. In contrast, a work-ready institution has a more service-oriented institutional logic. Knowledge and education are focused on work, workers and industry needs. Also, these institutions rely on market demand for their outputs as a form of governance. The idea of universities as institutions to help develop and drive a knowledge economy elevates work-ready above life-ready. In contrast, when universities want to engineer a better society, they chart a course for the moral high ground. However, what they might find here is that this is a very expensive and contested piece of real estate. In Australia much of the commentary about public university strategy reflects the tension between these three institutional logics. So the way that this tension is papered over is for many institutions to proclaim that they embrace all three logics. This they hope will provide some New World mojo with some Old World respect.

The theory of a university guides its telos or mission to use the corporate jargon?[4] The contemporary social philosopher Jonathan Haidt argues that a university can have only one telo, and this must be truth (aka enlightenment, reason, wisdom). Others like industry engagement or social justice are at best a distraction, and at worst, they produce institutional incoherence and internal conflict. Love him or hate him (and many people do), Jonathan Haidt brings up a crucial strategic issue for universities, namely, what is their mission?

Some recent advertising at MIT paraphrased the institution's mission as discover / educate. For many other universities it is expressed as research, which is then used as a foundation for teaching/education. In this section we will characterise universities according to their relative emphasis on four missions—research, education, engagement and the emerging issue of social justice. A university where research leads will be called an Intellectual Capital organisation. One where education leads is called an Information Dissemination organisation. One where engagement leads is called a Responsive organisation. And one where social justice leads is called a Social Equity organisation. While these characterisations are somewhat crude, they are useful to highlight potential institutional incoherence and resulting institutional complexity.

One reason why some of these missions clash with, or at least have a strained relationship with each other, is that they produce different outcomes from a university. For example, research and education are designed to privilege one section of society—the university graduates, at the expense of the non-graduates—whose tax dollars help to fund the universities. And when work and education focus on the knowledge economy, industry becomes a privileged partner. In contrast, social justice is designed to create equality and fairness and fund the disadvantaged. Here universities try to shape the notion of what is meant by good citizenship. However, as the global financial crisis and the Australian Banking Royal Commission illustrated, in key sectors of the knowledge economy, many companies and their senior managers (aka graduates) do not agree with, or practice, the social justice moral codes promoted by universities.

In a harsh light, a university degree is a 'positional good'.[5] It provides graduates with a social advantage such as access to a range of better (higher-paying) jobs and membership of the graduate 'club' of the universities. Also, if knowledge is power and this helps to create a meritocracy, then university research and its related knowledge and education can be characterised as creating winners and losers. From this perspective university social justice programmes can be framed as a reaction to the success of segmenting society. And university social welfare programmes, like scholarships for underprivileged students, can be characterised as a social tax paid by these institutions for their social license to operate.

In the corporate world the idea that 'bad' companies pay a social tax through their corporate social responsibility programmes is common. For example, all the financial institutions paraded before the Australian Banking Royal Commission for their 'bad' behaviour had extensive corporate social responsibility programmes. These banks knew that their business models were designed to provide benefits to large numbers of people. But they also knew that their operations exploited large numbers of people (customers) for the benefit of smaller groups of people (staff and shareholders). So they are comfortable paying a corporate tax to government and a social tax to special groups.

Our point is not to criticise the motivation or content of the social justice and welfare programmes that are becoming more prevalent in universities. Our point is to suggest that it is easy to reframe this activity as a cynical exercise of institutional behaviour. We also believe that it is a source of institutional complexity, which, in turn, is a root cause of muddled strategy.

7.2 The Missions of Australia's Universities

The University of Melbourne's strategy statement positions the institution as an Intellectual Capital organisation. The strategy story told in the document leads with research, which flows into pedagogy and then into community service. It is clear that the university wants to be known first and foremost as a research-led institution with the goal of being rated as such in various world reputation rankings. It will be held publicly accountable, and hostage to its relative performance. Our interpretation of the strategy story is that pedagogy is very important, but its quality will not be measured in the same harsh light as research. Thus, because both public and private measures like individual KPIs drive actions more than aspirations, research trumps teaching and learning. Finally, the university aspires to being known as a 'public-spirited university'. Exactly what this means is unclear.

The University of Newcastle also has a three-part mission, but its emphasis and language are more diffuse than those of the University of Melbourne. Its vision/strategy statement leads with its 'enduring commitment to equity and social justice'. Then comes 'graduates who make a difference',; 'a passion for excellence and discovery', 'driving global and regional impact', 'engaging across the globe', 'a shared future with our communities', 'staff who make their mark' and, finally, 'building a sustainable future'. All these from a small regional university that is probably best known for its Faculty of Health and Medicine. The final section of *The New Futures Strategic Plan 2016–2025* talks about the indigenous artist whose paintings decorate the strategy statement. The University of Newcastle looks like a Social Equity organisation.

Like the University of Newcastle, the University of Technology Sydney (UTS) strives to be excellent across teaching, research, community service and social justice. However, its social aspirations seem more pervasive than many of its peers. The vice chancellor once stated to one of us that his aim was for UTS to help create a socially just, equitable and inclusive society for all people. To do this it would be a public institution of exemplary social behaviour. As the leader of such an institution, the vice chancellor gives some of his salary back to the university as a scholarship fund. And to become such a model institution, the university offers seminars on implementing its values, such as integrity in teaching and research. It also requires mandatory training for all staff on issues such as equal opportunity, mental health awareness, privacy essentials, communication and collaboration, consent (unwanted sexual behaviour), health and safety, legal affairs, preventing bullying, and safety and well-being. And it has just negotiated a workplace agreement that includes five days cultural and ceremonial leave per year for indigenous Australian staff. While many people are proud of these initiatives, others are more circumspect about their prominence.

From a strategic perspective what is interesting about the UTS workplace agreement is a clause that provides a provision for 20 days paid leave per year for staff subject to domestic violence. This is a provision that has nothing to do with the UTS work environment. So here the institution is quietly crossing from a social justice mission to a social welfare mission. The university is edging towards becoming a Social Welfare organisation.

Finally, as two old business school professors, the University of South Australia (UniSA) strategy caught our attention. UniSA wants to be known as a business and industry-oriented university. In its *Enterprise25* strategic plan (2018–2025) the vice chancellor's overview suggests that by 'taking an industry sector approach' the university's teaching will be 'industry informed' and its research will be 'inventive and adventurous'. Hence, 'the world should look to UniSA for innovation'. Searching the strategy document reveals that the university hopes to generate 10% of its operational income from industry partners and 'teaching, research and practice will be consolidated on precincts closely integrated and aligned with industry'. Industry partners will inform curriculum and provide internships so that 'students continue to graduate with above average career outcomes'. This approach characterises a Responsive organisation. Here is a university that wants to establish capabilities to respond to the needs of business and industry.

Being an Information Dissemination university seems to be a required position for all universities. The storyline here is that education is extremely important. While some universities lead with education, they quickly follow with research and often social justice in the institution's strategy narrative. So Information Dissemination becomes the anchor point, and the other three teloi are used to extend this fundamental purpose. Because Jonathan Haidt argues that social justice is a dangerous telos, we now look at why this might be the case.

7.3 The Social Justice Mission

There are two aspects to university-inspired social justice. One is an internal utopian attitude about how a university should work. Consider the vision of Professor John Fischetti, the dean of the School of Education at the University of Newcastle:[6]

> If we come together as leaders in a community of well-being, kindness and keenness to solve problems and create knowledge in flexible ways, using emerging smart tools to reinforce learning, we can fully embrace the opportunities and challenges of the interconnected world.

It is hard to argue with such a vision.

The second aspect of social justice concerns the university's leadership and outreach. Here the mission is to be perceived as a moral and ethical organisation. The problem here is that this is often a journey across contested ground. And, in a multicultural society that welcomes students from many different countries it is hard to gauge social mores and get a balance that does not offend a particular group. Also, because the idea of social justice is ill-defined, it is easy for many different concerns to be corralled into this mission. Here are some examples of the difficulties of being a leading social justice institution.

- To recognise the plight of indigenous Australians, many of our universities make a symbolic gesture to these people by stating an Acknowledgement of Country in their public strategy document and before important meetings. However, such symbolism and similar statements of support for a range of social issues such as for marriage equality and against domestic violence can easily open the door to the invasion of identity politics into a university. Some people suggest that some of these issues have become weaponised by advocate groups as a means of bullying opponents into silence.
- A recent case about a professor at James Cook University provides a good example of advocacy groups and intellectual bullying.[7] Professor Peter Ridd's outspoken criticism of the quality of the research concerning the health of the Great Barrier Reef in Australia angered some colleagues and many reef advocacy groups. To placate these groups, the university then made up a number of spurious charges about his general conduct as an academic and terminated his employment. This case gained international attention and crowdfunding and went to the Federal Court which ruled that his termination was unlawful. In this case two fundamental issues were highlighted by Justice Vasta. The first relates to the concept of intellectual freedom, which he noted that

the university administrators did not understand. He said that the concept was extremely important because it helped to define the mission of any university. 'Whilst it might not be a fundamental right, it is nonetheless the cornerstone upon which the university exists.' However, there are many instances where there is no mention of this fundamental value in the statements of strategy in Australia's universities. The second point the judge made related to the fallout of stating a contrarian view. He noted that '[i]n the search for truth, it is an unfortunate consequence that some people may feel denigrated, offended, hurt or upset. It may not always be possible to act collegiately when diametrically opposed views clash in the search for truth.' So the challenge for vice chancellors and all the members of a university is to tolerate alternative points of view.

- Social justice is an easy target for the media. For example, after it was alleged that the University of Sydney tried to suppress a report by John Mack and Rachel Wilson on the low tertiary admission standards of students entering teaching degrees, the media had a field day criticising the University of Sydney and other universities for the fall in standards.[8] Journalists were happy to use intellectual entry standards as a moral imperative—a society can't afford to have poor teachers. Even some politicians expressed their dismay. For example, Ross Stokes, the NSW Minister for Education, said that 'certain universities have lost sight of their social duty. Focused on the profits they make from cramming teaching degrees with as many students as possible, they view their ITE programs as income streams rather than training grounds for future educational leaders'.[9]
- Another danger with a social justice mission is that it is easy to choose a path to righteousness but much harder for its guides to be seen as above reproach. For example, as noted earlier, in 2018 one of the chief guides to help the University of Technology Sydney become a model social institution, namely the chancellor of the university, was also the chair of the board of the Commonwealth Bank—an institution whose reputation was savaged by the Royal Commission into Misconduct in the Banking, Superannuation and Financial Services Industry. Members of the council of the university seemed to be unaware or unconcerned about the symbolism of the head of what the media were

saying was an unethical organisation also being the head of an institution striving to be a model social institution.

- Because social justice is a difficult concept to pin down, it will inevitably mean different things to different people. So when an organisation adopts this mission, what happens is that powerful or loud supporters promote their likes and dislikes.[10] These then become the focus for a portfolio of programmes to address these issues. And as programmes are added, so the requirement for administrative support rises and costs increase. Without new external funding, these programmes take money away from education and research.

So why has social justice and its bedfellow political correctness materialised and why is it consolidating in many universities? As we noted earlier, the implementation of the NPM regime in universities has motivated them to remember their public service origins. One easy way to do this is to be seen as energetic about public issues. Another reason is that as more people attend university from a variety of backgrounds, they bring with them a greater variety of identity issues and concerns. In the pluralist organisation of a university these ideas are tolerated and often welcomed. To complement this situation, in recent years there has been a social movement to explicitly recognise and accommodate diversity in all its forms. Thus, social justice and political correctness have found a friendly home.

From a strategic perspective the social justice narrative is that respecting and addressing these concerns enhance the citizenship reputation of the university. The risk here is that because reputation is a bipolar evaluation, it can be enhanced or degraded by the actions of a university. So aggressively promoting a social justice agenda is a two-edged sword—get out of step with, or too far in front of society, and one's reputation can be damaged. A second problem with investing in social justice to enhance the institution's citizenship reputation was noted earlier. This aspect of university operations is not captured in the reputation ranking systems in which most universities strive to excel.

To its critics social justice is an imposed mindset, or a form of social engineering in the culture of a university. Because many of these political ideas are contested by different groups of stakeholders, this mission has the capacity to add hidden social and economic costs to the university. To many readers this may sound like a harsh evaluation. But what research in the corporate sector has illustrated is that some of the most strident advocates of social responsibility have used this persona as a smokescreen for their nefarious business practices.[11] Enron was a poster example. On its journey to bankruptcy and membership in the unethical Hall of Fame it received many awards for its corporate social responsibility. At a broader level, trying to help engineer the social fabric of Australia is a much more obscure aspiration than focusing on the observed benefits from helping to create a better knowledge-based economy.

The discussion so far in this chapter raises a number of related strategic questions for every university. First, should an Australian public university seek to achieve excellence across more than one mission or a set of related missions? What internal tensions (institutional incoherence) might the pursuit of dissonant missions raise? Do multiple missions add unnecessary complexity to the university? Could a university fulfil its obligations to the Grand Bargain by focusing primarily on a single dominant mission?

7.4 Multiple Missions

The previous discussion has been purposefully vague about university missions. Here, we sharpen the discussion by describing four missions for a university—knowledge creation, knowledge dissemination, community and industry engagement, and social justice. The aim is to highlight areas of similarity and difference. If the differences outweigh the similarities, this suggests institutional incoherence. The strategic principal at play here is 'focus'. Many of the best organisations in the world have a single 'dominant logic' that guides how they integrate their mission, vision and values.

So, what defines and differentiates each mission?

- ***Knowledge Creation***—a Scholarship—Endowment Game
  - Emphasis on the unfiltered pursuit of knowledge; scholars and the university protect scientific values

- External money from government and industry is available to fund thinking
- International reputation is based on interesting and impactful ideas, and star academics
- Reputation attracts endowments from alumni and people wanting to fund important thinking
- Economies of scope across research areas (breakthroughs in one area feed better thinking in other areas) are more important than economies of scale (spreading the fixed costs of facilities and labour) within a research area
- A vibrant PhD programme is a loss leader for research and a key investment in future reputation
- Staff have low teaching loads relative to colleagues in Information Dissemination universities
- The centre of gravity of the institution is research and postgraduate programmes
- Universities are guardians of intellectual standards and intellectual integrity
- The primary consumers of the intellectual capital generated by the university is the world-wide academic community
- Clear measures of success are available (such as journal publications, academic citations and PhD completions)
- Private benefits accrue to individual researchers and the host university; public benefits accrue to people and organisations that use the research
- Some low-cost degree programmes allow teaching to cross-subsidise research
- Alumni and research endowments are important.

• ***Information Dissemination***—an Education—Fee for Service Game

  - Students, teaching and related infrastructure are the first priority
  - Learning values such as engaging and challenging students drive the design and delivery of stare-of-the-art courses
  - Production of information and student learning of basic material drive efficiency

- Local reputation based on easy access, teaching excellence and programme relevance
- Local reputation attracts local praise and student scholarships
- Large student numbers in the core programmes drive cost recovery
- Mix of low- and high-cost degree programmes allows for cross-subsidies across the programmes
- Staff have higher teaching loads than their colleagues in knowledge creation universities
- Process improvements in programme design and delivery drive staff and student 'hygiene' satisfaction
- The centre of gravity of the institution is undergraduate teaching
- The primary consumers of the intellectual capital of the university are graduates and their employers
- Clear measures of success are available such as student satisfaction and jobs after graduation
- Private benefits accrue to graduates through higher wages and public benefits to government through higher taxes paid by the graduates
- Because student fees cover operating costs, growth generates free cash flow.

• ***Community and Industry Engagement***—a Social and Economic Improvement—Internal Subsidy Game

- Staff and students are encouraged to participate in outreach activities
- University infrastructure is a community resource
- Universities host community forums and events
- Universities maintain archives and museums
- Relationships between Town and Gown are important
- Input into government policy is encouraged
- Enhancing civic knowledge and responsibility is a university responsibility
- Collaboration with business and industry is encouraged
- Special groups are identified and programmes created to meet their needs
- Measures of success are based more on participation than measurable outcomes

- Private benefits accrue to people and organisations that engage directly with the university; public benefits accrue to the local community
- Costs of these activities are largely hidden within university budgets.

• ***Social Justice and Equity***—a Sociopolitical Fairness and Welfare Game[12]

- Emphasis on social values such as integrity, inclusiveness, ethics, diversity, equity, opportunity and creating a welcoming work environment
- Social values are transmitted throughout the organisation by seminars, training, affirmative action programmes and workplace agreements
- The university is not afraid to take a stance on social issues
- Universities are guardians of social mores; they project and protect these values
- The university creates an environment that fosters the development of human quality, such that graduates and staff are expected to be people who possess ethical, civic, political and social responsibilities
- Teaching and research involve moral judgements about selecting students, transmitting certain types of knowledge and selecting research topics
- Reputation revolves around being seen as a model public institution
- Staff and students are required to commit to the institution's core values
- Because social justice is such a multifaceted concept, the programmes supported by powerful people represent the centre of gravity of the institution
- The primary beneficiaries of the university's actions are its members, alumni and specific community groups
- Targeted programmes are used to signal human qualities and a sense of justice
- Costs are largely hidden within university budgets.

The Value of Community Service

Community relationships, aka Town and Gown, have a long history in university life. As universities grow, they often come to define, and sometimes dominate, their local communities. However, at particular times of the year, their presence can be quite disruptive. So there is often a tension between (small) Town and (big) Gown.

Because a university sits in a social and industrial community and people from these communities supply resources to it and work within the university, it makes strategic sense for the relationship between Town and Gown to be nurtured. A payoff for many of the communities is the employment generated by the university. Another is to be identified with their universities—such as Boston with Harvard, MIT and Boston University; Silicon Valley with Stanford, UC Berkeley and UC San Francisco, and Oxford and Cambridge in the UK.

7.5 Combining Multiple Missions into a Single Strategy

After looking at many statements of strategy, we think that most of these seem to have been constructed by picking elements from each of the four missions. By jumbling aspects of these together, they hope to create a more inclusive university. However, designing a strategy to build institutional coherence from a mixture of missions will be a challenging task. Also, the mixed nature of the elements ensures that the many and varied operational procedures necessary to deliver the outcomes associated with each element will be complex. So is it possible to develop a coherent strategy from a mixed-mission model? Here is a somewhat convoluted storyline that incorporates all the elements.

Let's assume that the core concept of a university's strategy is to stimulate, enhance, grow and serve the knowledge economy. And that the existing faculties will be used as the primary vehicles for implementation. Here, research can be seen as an upstream activity for education as well as a free-standing output. Education and research are complementary inputs to enhancing the knowledge economy, especially if education is informed by research. Industry engagement can be seen as an input to research and teaching (e.g., by funding and scholarships) and/or a guide to these activities (e.g., by articulating innovation and educational needs). Community engagement provides a set of enabling relationships by supporting the operations of the institution with local resources. Social justice acts as a moral guide to resource procurement, operations and the establishment of graduate attributes. And a Grand Bargain that suggests that the four missions are equally important also suggests that many different groups of stakeholders are equally important—staff, students, alumni, industry, the local community and global citizens.

So how might such a university work? Ulrich Pidun and his colleagues suggest that organisations tend to reap the rewards of such diversification when they take three steps:[13]

1. Limit the number of business models in the portfolio of business units / faculties. As discussed earlier, these business models refer to knowledge creation (via research), knowledge dissemination (via education and engagement) and social justice (via internal values and engagement). The faculties operationalise the first two functions, while central administration guides the last function. Research and education can and should cross-pollinate each other. As Fig. 7.1 later suggests, it is the social justice ideal and its business model that adds little direct value to the outputs of the other two activities.
2. Tailor the corporate parenting strategy to the portfolio of business units. In universities, the role of the parent is contingent on what it sees as the roles of its faculties, as shown in Fig. 4.4 (Chap. 4). Depending on which quadrant a faculty resides in, it needs different types and levels of support from the central administration of the university. Also, the capabilities of the parent play a key role in helping or hindering the operations of the faculties. Too much, or inefficient, bureaucratic 'support' from the parent can easily hinder the operations of a faculty.
3. Allocate resources based on clear portfolio roles. In universities most resource allocation will occur via capital allocations, establishing staffing levels, internal revenue sharing (tax) levels and through activity-based (and sometimes performance-based) budgets. The key

strategic issue here is to be clear about which faculties are designated as development, growth, base or harvesting units. Or to be slightly more blunt, which faculties are the cash cows that generate revenue for others to use. A key problem for many universities is that their faculties have no clear role in the portfolio.

There are, however, a number of requirements for a multiple-mission guide to strategy to 'work'. The first is that the strategy narrative must be coherent and persuasive. The one above is more like a jigsaw puzzle than a good story. Also, the parts of the strategy identified in Fig. 4.3 must be aligned. To achieve this, there must be direct, measurable, personally accountable lines-of-sight from each mission to the core concept of strategy. These will be institutionalised in the university's budgets and organisation-wide protocols. They will also be operationalised by the faculties. For example, if a faculty seeks to embrace social justice, how might social justice 'infect' teaching, course content and research? A common approach is to offer a course in ethics. This inevitably raises questions of which ethics (say Eastern or Western; and then maybe virtue, deontology or consequentialism) and how they should be taught? Also, should the course be compulsory? And when should it be taught—early or late in a programme? So assuming that the course has been taken, it is then left up to the students and staff to apply a set of ethics or an ethical framework in their work and life. More likely than not, like most other such courses, many staff and students will compartmentalise this material rather than let it infect every aspect of other courses and their (work) life.

Now consider research. It must be clear and measurable how a piece of academic research has been informed by the needs of industry or society or social justice and how it has responded to these needs. Also needed would be a procedure or metric to show how this research has informed some aspect of student education. Then academics would need to be held accountable for hitting or missing such outcomes, as would their supervisors. The empty clichés found in many statements of strategy fail this test. They suggest that the social justice mission of most universities is bolted-on rather than built-in to the strategy.

The built-in approach of industry engagement was illustrated by the practice of the Harvard Business School. Here, the dominant form of research is clinically based, qualitative, field research. The academics visit companies and study how they perform. This research is then used to write case studies that are used in all the teaching programmes. Faculty are rewarded and promoted for this research and case writing. The faculty who write the cases teach the classes. The paradox here is that because most other business schools reward discipline-based theoretical and empirical research, an academic from the Harvard Business School has far fewer job opportunities outside Harvard than most other academics.

A second problem with a multiple-mission approach is that there is no indication of what is most important, who is most important and what the university will not do. While it is 'politically' safe not to single out any function or group as most important, it is strategically naïve to assume that everything is important because strategy choices inevitably involve trade-offs across functions and groups of people. Also, it helps everybody in the university and the community to know what the university will not do and why.

Many strategists suggest that for an organisation to seek to fulfil multiple, largely independent missions is a recipe for misadventure. The evidence for this opinion is that many conglomerates comprised of unrelated businesses have found it difficult to compete with more specialised or more focused competitors. The strategy consulting firm McKinsey & Company notes that most universities are designed as diversified conglomerates or as others have called them comprehensive universities, aka the multiversity. They are made up of many largely independent strategic business units—faculties with schools and departments and research centres.[14]

One rationale for aggregating unrelated faculties in a single university is that the fortunes and misfortunes of particular faculties offset each other—like the finance idea of portfolio diversification. A second rationale is that growth is easy to pursue. It can be achieved by adding more academic units such as the currently fashionable artificial intelligence and big data analytics. Also, if a new sociopolitical concern emerges, it can be accommodated by adding a new area of education or a specialist research centre, such as the rush by most universities into the indigenous education arena.

Some conglomerates have a strategic logic other than portfolio diversification, namely, the structure is based on the idea of horizontal or vertical diversification. Here integration is sought across related, but parallel, disciplines such as pharmacology, medicine and dentistry (horizontal diversification), or upstream and downstream disciplines like chemistry, biology and pharmacology (vertical diversification). In either case the idea is to seek out synergies across faculties beyond that of merely sharing infrastructure. There is some evidence to suggest that well-managed horizontal or vertically integrated conglomerates are viable structures.[15] But as we will see later, most universities are organised as a set of silos that don't really want to engage with each other.

Another way to think strategically about if and how multiple missions might inform a coherent core strategy is to construct a value chain. Value chain diagrams map how the major parts of a university might be organised and integrated to deliver the telos of a university. The idea here is that different parts of the university create different types of outcomes that come together to provide some clear overall value to society.

7.6 The Value Chain of a University

The value-chain model in Fig. 7.1 is for a hypothetical university. The top of the diagram suggests that knowledge reputation is a key summary of a university's achievements, in this case, for how it will enhance the knowledge economy. At the bottom of the value chain we see how the key factors of production support the various chains of value creation. Here funding (aka, the economic logic or business model) anchors all the other activities. It fuels research (time and infrastructure), recruitment (via salaries and student course fees), infrastructure (the campus, information technology and other administrative services) and marketing (done by the university and its agents). Hence, how to ensure sufficient and sustainable funding is the key priority. Without a cogent business model, a university effectively limps from year to year. The great universities of the world help to insure against this problem by establishing and managing a large endowment.[16]

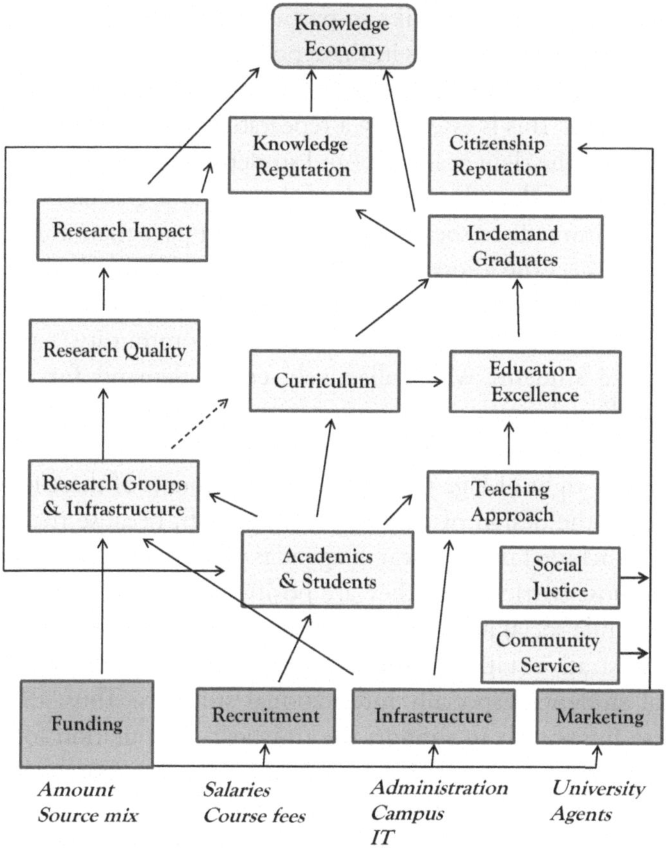

Fig. 7.1 University value chain

On the left side of Fig. 7.1 is a knowledge creation value chain. This is essentially an innovation process. Funding pays for research (groups) who do quality research that is noticed and used, which in turn creates reputation for the university. If the university's research groups are organised around solving a vexing problem, and if they do quality research that makes breakthroughs (impact), this will make a more immediate economic impact than if the university scatters its research agenda haphazardly across many different facilities. Knowledge reputation also flows back to attract the next generation of academics and students. This helps explain why vice chancellors like to participate in the rankings and promote their institution's success in these polls.

The centre and right side of Fig. 7.1 map an information dissemination value chain. This is essentially a repeatable process. Here, the necessity is to recruit the right academics and students and design a curriculum to continually produce in-demand graduates. The graduates will then have a more immediate social and economic impact than a curriculum designed to reflect the idiosyncratic interests of particular academics. The pivot point of both the knowledge creation and information dissemination value chains is the university's academic community, namely, the staff and the students who collectively create demand for university research and teaching.

The community service and social justice perspectives are also included in the bottom-right of Fig. 7.1. While some elements of these may influence parts of the design of teaching and research, because the concerns are seldom included in the research agendas of academics, nor embedded deeply in most curriculums, they are positioned as free-standing activities. Also, while social justice policies may resonate with many academics and administrative staff, it is not clear how they resonate with different groups of students, especially international students. Thus, the role of both these missions is to support the university's reputation for citizenship. A problem here is that it is not clear how a university's citizenship reputation advances the knowledge economy.

While each university will be a particular version of the model in Fig. 7.1, the process of constructing such a value chain is a useful way to identify key resources and capabilities, and where the crucial nodes in the network of value creating activities are located. For example, if the University of New South Wales replaced the 'knowledge economy' outcome at the top of Fig. 7.1 with 'Australia's Global University', they could then design the chains of value-creating activities needed to create a world-class global university. For example, in the Curriculum 'box' there might be a specialisation on courses that have a common global core of knowledge. There might also be reference to the study of the languages, cultures and legal systems of Australia's major trading partners. And there might be a new box inserted in the diagram to reflect the various international alliances that a global university will have. Without such a road map it is extremely difficult to understand some of the key aspects of UNSW's strategy and how these combine to achieve its grand vision. This type of strategic design is doubly useful if it is also done to profile the university's major local competitor, namely, the University of Sydney.

From a strategic perspective a value chain map like Fig. 7.1 provides both a tool for understanding strategy and a storyboard for discussing strategy. What factors are included and omitted, how those that are included interact and which of these attract investment, summarise many of the key choices made by the institution's strategic planners. For example, in Fig. 7.1, there is only one dashed cross-over arrow where research enhances teaching to co-create in-demand graduates. This suggests low integration.[17] And, if the institution's culture and/or organisational design (such as its faculty silos) also limit integration, it would suggest that there are really two parallel universities embedded in Fig. 7.1—one for knowledge creation (which is an innovation, batch-processing operation) and one for information dissemination (which is a continuous-processing operation). Thus, the main reason for including both in the same institution is for one to cross-subsidise the other—teaching pays for research.

Value chain diagrams like Fig. 7.1 also suggest where the institution should develop specific internal capabilities. For example, because academics and students are a pivot point for the university profiled here, we would expect to be able to find a clear set of integrated programmes to recruit, develop and retain key academics, and other programmes to recruit, educate and get employment for the targeted types of students. Most published statements of strategy are largely silent on these issues. Some say that they are investing in recruitment or increasing the size of the academic and student cohorts, but it is difficult to find a university that provides a clear explanation of its human resource strategy. Professional service firms tend to provide much better information on attaining and retaining this key resource than our universities.

7.7 The Big Strategic Choice

The discussion in this chapter poses the following choices for a university:

- Cherry-pick aspects from the four missions, or
- Pick a single mission, or
- Design an integrated multi-part mission (like research-led pedagogy) without any added extras?

As noted earlier, many current strategies look like a version of the cherry-picking option. They are easy to sell to all the stakeholders of a university because they speak to each group. They purposively exclude nobody. They are 'politically correct' in their content and tone of voice. They speak to their Grand Bargain with the government. They require only incremental change. But they pose some significant challenges to gaining greater efficiency and effectiveness. And they look muddled from a strategic point of view.

Alternatively, could an existing university realistically focus on a single mission, such as education only or research and doctoral training? What might this entail? First, it would take courage to try. Then it would involve a choice of what mission to adopt. And then it would take a coherent strategy to design and implement. Part of this strategy would entail some significant changes to the structure of the university, like closing some parts and reallocating resources to the chosen areas. There would be some happy winners and very angry losers!

A different type of focus might be to embrace serving selected parts of the knowledge economy. The university would address the needs of a specific industry and its work and workers. It would be guided by the philosophy of creating 'work-ready' and thus 'in-demand' graduates. Vertical integration would motivate the design of its operational units. NPM ideas could be used to manage the institution. It would be driven by demand—of students and industry. It would be an entrepreneurial responsive institution.

Another type of focus might be to adopt the mission of creating 'life-ready' citizens or helping social welfare institutions. Target students might be potential diplomates, civil servants, civic leaders, union leaders, politicians, media people, social workers, aid workers, teachers, managers of non-government, civil society and not-for-profit organisations. Operational units, curriculum and educational practices might be quite novel. Access would be open to a variety of people. It could be a Social Justice and Equity university.

However, the most likely path for most universities is to choose a multi-part mission. For example, the Group-of-Eight universities suggest that this is their preferred position. Their statements of strategy suggest that research-led education is the dominant mission. Looking across the statements of strategy of this group, we see reference to a university that many older academics would recognise. It seeks to adopt the Humboldt model of a community of scholars that creates and disseminates knowledge. It will guard the ethics of science and education. It will be guided by its scientific compass and the value of scientific inquiry. Education is informed by research. It will uphold academic freedom. It will be organised around discipline and cross-discipline faculties. It will focus on supply—of new knowledge and scientists. It will try to lead demand by shaping the knowledge base of its graduates and the focus of industry. It will adopt some NPM management ideas to enhance efficiency and effectiveness. It will be an elite intellectual capital institution of excellence.

But the current reality is that research competes with relevance as the guiding force for what is taught in the classroom, and relevance rather than scientific curiosity is what attracts most research money. Also, when the academic freedom of a person or group is challenged by a noisy group, the commitment of the senior executive is more than likely to bend to the noise. And then the universities keep adding extra policies and programmes into an already cluttered workspace. They look more like the platforms of political party than a well-run institution. Many universities are also disturbed by the latest consulting ideas or technology breakthroughs. Finally, as we illustrate in Chap. 11 their organisation designs are confused and confusing.

Notes

1. Available at http://www.anu.edu.au/news/all-news/Vice-Chancellor-speech-To-the-World-Academic-Summit.
2. Aristotle often evaluated a thing with regard to its telos—its purpose, end or goal.
3. See, for example, S. Oertel and M. Söll, "Universities between Traditional Forces and Modern Demands: The Role of Imprinting on the Missions of German Universities", *Higher Education*, Vol. 73 (2017), 1–18.
4. J. Haidt, "Why Universities Must Choose One Telos: Truth or Social Justice". Downloaded from http://heterodoxacademy.org/2016/10/21/one-telos-truth-or-social-justice/
5. F. Hirsch, *Social Limits to Growth* (London: Routledge, 1977).
6. J. Fischetti, "The three things universities must do to survive disruption", *The Conversation* (19 June, 2019).
7. G. Lloyd, "Free to Defy Orthodoxy", *The Australian*, (18 April, 2019), 11.
8. N. Robinson, "Students with lowest ATAR scores being offered places in teaching degrees: secret report", ABC News (18 September, 2018).
9. R. Stokes, "How universities lower teacher standards by focusing on profit", *Sydney Morning Herald* (20 September, 2018), p. 25.
10. Interestingly, people who are against a social justice issue seldom lobby for it not to be recognised.
11. See for example, J. Chen, D. Patten and R. Roberts, "Corporate Charitable Contributions: A Corporate Social Performance or Legitimacy Strategy?" *Journal of Business Ethics*, Vol. 82, No. 1 (2008), 131–144; D. Prior, J. Surroca and J. Tribo, "Are Socially Responsible Managers Really Ethical? Exploring the Relationship between Earnings Manipulation and Corporate Social Responsibility", *Corporate Governance*, Vol. 16, No. 3 (2008), 160-177. Also, it is from the corporate sector that universities now recruit some senior executives.
12. The Spanish Jesuit universities are good examples of this type of university. Their social justice orientation is grounded in their spirituality, and they try to embed this in campus life.
13. U. Pidun, A. Richter, M. Schommer and A. Karna, "A New Playbook for Diversified Companies", *MIT Sloan Management Review*, Vol. 60, No. 2 (2018).
14. B. T. Ferrari and P. H. Phan, "Universities and the Conglomerate Challenge" *McKinsey Quarterly* (September, 2018).

15. U. Pidun, A. Richter, M. Schommer and A. Karna, "A New Playbook for Diversified Companies", *MIT Sloan Management Review*, Vol. 60, No. 2 (2018).
16. For example, in 2015 some endowments were—Harvard $36.9 billion, Yale $23.6 billion, Stanford $17.2 billion, Princeton $16.4 billion and MIT 10.1 billion. The Harvard Management Company manages its endowment.
17. Even though research-active academics might design curriculum and do much of the teaching, this does not automatically mean that research informs teaching. For example, most of an undergraduate curriculum is based on 'old news' (the basics of a discipline), not 'new news' (latest research findings). The postgraduates will get more new news.

8

What Are the Strategies of Australia's Universities? Objectives

Because most university funding comes from government sources, one would expect that a basic objective of all these institutions would be to diversify their sources of revenue. The primary mechanisms to achieve this objective are to increase student fees, the institutional endowment, the return on university investments, and the return from research and decrease the costs of running the university. In some statements of strategy these objectives were mentioned; however, in many they were ignored. From a strategic perspective the interesting questions are as follows: What constitutes the optimum size for a particular university given its location and history? What percentage of independent funding offers it sufficient independence, and what are the risks of different types of funding and cost control? All these issues speak to the business model of the university. It is hard to find specific answers to these questions in most statements of strategy.

So what else do the universities seek to achieve?

Recall that the University of New South Wales has a grand vision to be 'Australia's global university'. This is its desired University of the Future. The vision is further elaborated as 'a global leader in discovery, innovation, impact and thought leadership' (p. 5 of the statement of strategy).

T. Devinney, G. Dowling, *The Strategies of Australia's Universities*,
https://doi.org/10.1007/978-981-15-3397-6_8

However, such a grand mission needs a set of specific goals to achieve its lofty aims. These contextualise and specify what needs to be achieved. In UNSW's strategy statement (page 7) it had ten goals, namely, (1) world-leading research, (2) research impact, (3) exemplary education, (4) in-demand graduates, (5) equity of opportunity, (6) thought leadership, (7) a significant contribution to national and global prosperity, (8) excellence in international education, (9) partnerships and (10) social justice. Because most Australian universities also strive to attain such goals, these are really points-of-parity, rather than points-of-difference. And most importantly, how do they combine to produce 'Australia's global university'?

To make things more complex than they need to be, for each of these ten broad goals UNSW has its own set of more specific objectives (three to five) and measures of performance. Recall that Chap. 1 suggested that objectives should focus on running today, building tomorrow and protecting the institution. They should also be measurable. So how do UNSW's objectives compare against these criteria? As expected, some are better than others, but none are specific enough to actually measure progress, and nowhere is a person or unit within the university identified as being responsible for meeting the target. For example, research progress will be measured by the university's 'ranking in the QS, ARWU and THES world university tables' (page 14). These were the rankings discussed in Chap. 4. But to be a meaningful goal, the reader needs to know why they were chosen, what the current ranking is, what the target ranking is and who will be praised or punished for (non)performance. Just doing better than last year is a bit vague.

The strategy statement also notes that each faculty of the university is tasked with pursuing all the goals/objectives noted earlier. So to implement this task, UNSW has a 'Strategic Matrix' (on page 10) that says that every faculty must deliver every 'priority and theme'. It also states that the 8 faculties, 1 college and 50 schools will work across 'the organizational structure and disciplines'. Does anybody really expect these silos to work together? The matrix then includes reference to three 'enablers', namely, people and culture, organisational effectiveness and sustainability and world-class environments. So here we see complexity—ten goals each to be delivered by an interconnected organisational structure of 51 operating units. Other big Australian universities are similarly complex, or to be less polite, similarly confused and confusing.

When goals are presented as a laundry list, they pose three strategic challenges. One is how to trade off competing priorities. The second is what to focus on. The third is what should the university really be known for. A bit more simplicity would help to overcome these challenges. For example, UNSW's ten goals can be easily collapsed into three, namely:

- Research—(6) thought leadership underpinned by (1) world-leading research that has (2) impact and that makes (7) a significant contribution to national and global prosperity.
- Education—(4) in-demand graduates developed through (8) excellence in international education, (3) exemplary education and (9) partnerships with other institutions.
- Social Justice (10)—delivered through (5) equity of opportunity.

So now the challenge for UNSW is to create a credible story for how achieving these three goals will coherently create a global university of distinction.

8.1 Local and More Operational Goals

If visionary goals seem a bit too generic, then it is worth searching for the more operational and local goals. For all its 'talk', UNSW and each of its local competitors in Sydney have one such operational goal that all members of its administrative team, all deans and all academics will agree on. It is probably one of the most important goals for the university. It is simply to get a higher share of the best school-leaving students. This is easily measurable each year. And it is hugely important because it drives a key part of the academic model of a university—good students help to produce good graduates. So where is this goal discussed in most strategy statements and what programmes are used to beat one's competitors? We know this goal and its associated programmes exist, but we could seldom find any discussion about this issue.

Most academics see their university's goals through the lens of their own performance and development key performance indicators (KPIs). Most administrators see the university goals through the lens of a budget or the objectives of a specific programme. These operational goals are much more practical than those stated in the published statement of strategy. Thus, they are much more likely to drive behaviour than their visionary counterparts. For example:

- One of the goals of the Alumni Office at Harvard University was once stated to one of us as 'to be the first of the third choices of a donor'.
- A goal of the old Australian Graduate School of Management (AGSM) was to be the first choice of domestic students who could not go overseas for their MBA.
- A goal of a regional university that interviewed one of us for the dean's job of their business school was stated as to get better performance out of its academic staff so they could rise up the rankings of the ERA.

Consider the Harvard University goal. What the Alumni Office at Harvard knew about getting people to donate to a university was that many people liked to give their money to a winning university because they thought it would be well spent by the university. Here, Harvard's reputation was a distinct advantage. What the managers also understood was that a rich person has a hierarchy of causes for their surplus money. First was their family. Second was the person's favourite cause—guide dogs, homeless people, cancer research and so forth. Third was 'other'. So Harvard University wanted to be the preferred 'other' for this pool of third-tier donations. This meant that it was not only competing for donations with other universities, but it was competing with charities and other good causes. And finally, what the Harvard fundraisers knew is that many big donations come from people who have a monument or memorial purpose in view.[1] Naming something after the donor is a key success factor here. So being 'first of the thirds' sounds sensible, and it provides a guide for where to look for these pots of gold.

Consider the AGSM goal to attract MBA students to a full-time two-year degree. In their business schools, most Australian universities want to attract more domestic students to get a good mix of local and international students. They also want to attract the best and brightest local students. This sounds like a great goal but it is not very realistic. Many of the very best business students go overseas for their education—they are supported by their parents or an overseas university scholarship. So the remaining pool of the best and brightest is quite limited. But there is a much larger pool of students who are very good but who will never be able to support themselves at an overseas university. So the AGSM and its principal competitor, the Melbourne Business School, both competed for 'the best of the seconds'. Both these schools also competed for the 'best of the seconds' in the market for company-sponsored short course executive education. The best and brightest managers were sent to Harvard Business School to attend one of their general manager programmes. This was perceived as a reward—yes, sent back to 'school' to work 12-hour days in a high-pressure educational environment with similar people from all over the world.

Consider the third goal of working the current academics harder. This is the implicit goal of many faculty deans in Australia's universities. The cohort of academic staff is largely fixed—in number and in quality; the terms of employment are also largely fixed, yet the university wants a quantum improvement in performance to appear in the next set of university rankings. One strategy is to set a number of stretch goals in the hope that at least some of them will be achieved. Another strategy is to 'raise the bar' of individual performance in the hope that the weak will leave and there are stronger people willing to take their place. Another strategy that some of the Chinese universities are using is to pay a significant financial performance bonus for achieving specific outcomes. However, it often takes years to rejuvenate and/or regenerate a cohort of academic staff. In reality, unlike the University of Newcastle's glowing appraisal of its staff, most of us are 'good but not great'. But nowhere in the public statements of strategy will you find an honest appraisal of staff quality. And from our experience, such a university-wide appraisal is difficult to find in the executive suite of our universities.

The argument against having 'sensible' or 'realistic' objectives is that they will not motivate significantly better performance. The alternative is to set 'stretch' objectives of the type found in the statements of strategy. These are supposed to be more inspiring. There is a vast scholarly goal-setting literature that speaks to this issue. It suggests caution! From a strategic perspective, the task is to make sure that there is a clear line-of-sight between the strategic objectives and the local objectives of individuals, faculties and administrative units.

8.2 Hoping for A While Rewarding B

To highlight the above aspect of strategic goal setting, we refer to an insightful paper written by Steven Kerr titled 'Hoping for A While Rewarding B'. Its thesis is that if you hope for A—such as getting the academics to publish impactful research that contributes to national and global prosperity, then you need to reward A, not B—which is something else.

In terms of research in the various business schools in which we spent most of our working lives, this principle was routinely violated. Most of the research that was highly praised had absolutely nothing to do with making an impact on the prosperity of anybody other than the academic whose name was on the publication. Teaching that was applauded in performance appraisals was based primarily on student satisfaction (or 'happy scores' as they were known) rather than what was actually learned and whether the curriculum was up to date and relevant. These KPIs motivated individuals to perform against a set of criteria that would get them promoted and receive salary supplementation. These were also the criteria that enhanced their academic reputation and thus gave them more market value and a portable CV. There was never a direct connection to the university's overall strategy, so most academics took little notice of it.

Another reason why there is often only a weak relationship between academic capabilities and what the university strategy desires in terms of creating 'impact' in society and the economy is that most recruiting is done by a faculty committee, not a university-wide committee. And for grades other than professors so is promotion. So what drives recruitment and the promotion of junior staff is local research customs and teaching demands. For example, if US-trained PhD graduates are believed to be better than Australian graduates, these are the ones recruited. If it is believed that employing them straight after graduation will secure the university's name on the publications that flow from their doctorate, then they are recruited immediately on graduation. So what we see is that many new academics enter the university with little or no teaching experience and no industry experience. It takes newly minted PhD graduates years to become proficient at their craft and to build the types of networks outside the university that will enable them to make the types of impact proudly proclaimed in the statements of strategy.

Hoping for A—changing the world for the better, while rewarding B—local excellence in teaching and the publication of research that speaks to a small number of academic colleagues reveals a major shortcoming of the strategies of most Australian universities. If a university really does want to make a direct and more immediate contribution to solving the challenges posed by the modern world, then it needs an academic cohort that has the motivation and capabilities to address these issues. Recruiting more (older) academically trained people who have experience in industry or public policy would be one approach. Hiring specific multi-disciplinary teams would be another approach.

Finally, there is an interesting reputation game invoked by the individual KPIs used by most Australian (and overseas) universities, especially those that drive research. Researchers are rewarded for high-quality research papers that enhance their own reputation.[2] In turn this reputation, especially when it grows to star status, enhances the marketability and commercial value of the individual. This often results in individuals holding their current institution hostage to the threat of being poached by another university. Many world-class researchers have been known to have major arguments about their worth to the university with their dean and vice chancellor. Because most of these arguments are 'reactive' in nature, it signals a lack of forethought by the senior executive of the university.

8.3 A Challenge

Here is a challenge for a university—to simplify its goals to provide a better line-of-sight between those of the institution and those of its staff.

If the local academic research goals focus mainly on getting published in discipline-based, top-rated, peer-reviewed journals, why not state that the research goal of the university is simply:

> To increase the stock of knowledge.[3]

If the goal of the education process is overwhelmingly to get students gainful employment, then the University of New South Wales goal may be all that is required, namely:

> To produce in-demand graduates.

Both these goals are simple and straightforward. They speak to running today, building tomorrow and protecting the (academic) reputation of the university. Also, they are easy to measure—for individuals, faculties and the university.

If the civic goal of the university is primarily to fulfil its responsibility to the Grand Bargain, then as the Australian Productivity Commission suggests (as noted in Chap. 1), each university might seek to be:

A well-functioning higher education institution that matches students with suitable study opportunities and meets the needs of the labour market. It should be open to people regardless of their background.

Here well-functioning means strategy-led and economy-focused.

Notes

1. One of our academic homes for a number of years at UTS, the Dr Chau Chak building designed by architect Frank Gehry is a good example of this.
2. University administrators might argue that these research papers enhance the reputation of the university. Yes, but not nearly as much as that of the individual. You can test this claim by asking people to name some of their favourite research papers and who were the authors, such as the Steven Kerr paper mentioned earlier. Then ask the person what journal the paper appeared in. Few will remember. Then ask them which university these

people were attached to at the time they published the paper. Most people will have no idea. For example, we have no idea, nor do we care where Steven Kerr was employed. Do you?

3. This was the goal articulated by Professor Brian Schmidt in his keynote address to the Times Higher Education Academic Summit in Singapore in 2018. Available at http://www.anu.edu.au/news/all-news/Vice-Chancellor-speech-to-the-World-Academic-Summit

9

What Are the Strategies of Australia's Universities? Arenas, Vehicles, Differentiators, Staging and Economic Logic

9.1 Arenas

Figure 7.1 earlier suggests that each of Australia's universities is probably two enterprises—one for education and the other for research. Each university differs somewhat according to the range of arenas (faculties) over which it practises these activities. For most universities their mix of faculties seems to be the result of circumstance as much as a grand design. In contrast, in the post-war years when Stanford University started its rise to stardom, the decision was made to concentrate on postgraduate programmes (where national reputations were forged), and a relatively few areas where government funding signalled national importance—one of which was electronics research. The aim was to do a few things with distinction rather than 'creating excellent programs in fields no one cares about'.[1]

A strategic decision that is very costly for a university is its choice of arenas. As just noted, Stanford chose some of these because the government of the day was prepared to underwrite much of the cost. If a university chooses to do world-class teaching and research in the natural and

T. Devinney, G. Dowling, *The Strategies of Australia's Universities*,
https://doi.org/10.1007/978-981-15-3397-6_9

physical sciences, it can involve significant investments in infrastructure. In contrast, research in many fields of the humanities is far less costly.

The number, variety and size of arenas define the scope and academic footprint of a university. From a strategic perspective, when the logic guiding the choice of arenas is not clear it

- makes positioning the institution more complicated,
- increases the costs of administration (due to complexity) and
- complicates decisions about which areas to prioritise for funding.

A criticism of Australia's public universities is that their scope is too broad. To illustrate this point, consider the profiles in Fig. 9.1. Each circle represents an academic faculty scaled to size. Their relationship is depicted by their distance from each other. An issue we will raise in Chap. 11 is that each of Australia's universities looks more like Comprehensive University, one with a scattered academic footprint, than Focused University where the logic of its collection of faculties is more apparent. And if the numerous research centres and institutes that a comprehensive university has were added to Fig. 9.1, the picture would look much more complex.

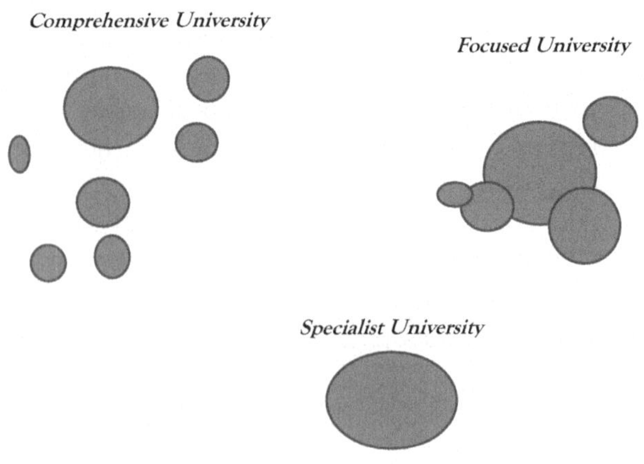

Fig. 9.1 Strategic scope

9.2 Vehicles

The major vehicles used to codify education, such as the common range of degrees; deliver education, such as teaching philosophy, curriculum design, lectures, tutorials and web-based materials; assess learning, such as assignments and examinations; and do research, such as academic time and research equipment, are similar across all of Australia's universities. Thus from both a student and an academic perspective, 'going to university' means that they are joining a fairly well-defined type of institution and committing to a broadly similar experience. Yes, each university has some unique aspects, but universities have a high degree of 'sameness'. The Vietnamese have a saying that captures this situation:

> Same, same, but different.

History and what is called isomorphism (imitation) create this sameness. This is the way that universities were organised in the past (history), and this is the way that a university's peers are currently organised, and so each tends to conform (isomorphism). Also, the rankings are designed to reflect this structure. So to look like a university, this is the dominant design. The value of this structuring of operations is that it clearly positions all universities as 'a university'. Stakeholders, both internal and external, are comfortable with this model. Consultants as we noted earlier suggest that it should be shattered.

It is interesting to delve deeper into the issue of sameness for two reasons. One is to expose the weakness of some consulting suggestions for change. At the present time many are simply infeasible. The other is to uncover the structural mechanisms that will impede any significant attempts to change.

9.3 Differentiators

Four institutional mechanisms cement the essential sameness of Australia's universities. The first is the overwhelming reliance on government funding. It is anchored to the Grand Bargain mentioned earlier, which comes with strings attached, namely, to be public institutions committed to the three traditional missions of teaching, research and community engagement. No university has the courage to publicly jettison any of these missions.

The second factor creating sameness is three powerful agencies. One is the Tertiary Education Quality and Standards Agency (TEQSA). Stemming from the Bradley Review of Australian Higher Education, this government regulator now imposes quality assurance mechanisms to set and review sector standards in the areas of teaching, learning, scholarship, research and research training. The second agency is the Australian Research Council's Excellence in Research Australia (ERA) programme. As noted earlier, this initiative produces an Australian university league table that encourages a degree of sameness of research across the universities by recognising discipline-based journal ranking lists which identify the set of de facto target journals for much university research. These are then used in the individual performance appraisal of staff. Thus, the requirements of these journals create the parameters for what is judged to be the type of research one should do and what quality means.

The third agency is the National Tertiary Education Union. This union negotiates the basic workplace agreements employed throughout the university system. While each university negotiates a different agreement with this powerful workforce union, they are very similar in structure and content. We would argue that these union agreements are designed more to protect the 'average' employee than to foster excellence across the system. One of their key conditions illustrates this opinion, namely, the duration of the paid working week. Currently this is typically 37.5 hours per week. For an academic 37.5 hours is far too short! It is impossible to be an excellent teacher and world-class researcher and then do some university service, and then some industry and community engagement by working 7.5 hours per day. So here is the problem:

- work 37.5 hours per week and do part of the job, or
- work 37.5 hours per week and do all the job at average quality or
- the university is deliberately underpaying its academic staff (and it should be taken to the Fair Work Commission).

When one of us first joined the Australian university system, our terms and conditions of employment would easily fit a 37.5 hours per week. The employment contract was one page in length. It had three main paragraphs:

1. Welcome to the university.
2. Your level is XYZ and your pay is $PQR pa.
3. If you have any questions please talk to your Head of School.

In essence, the deal was 'you pretend to work and we will pretend to pay you'. There were no formal university expectations (regular performance appraisals), and some academic staff treated their employment as a form of paid social welfare. And yes, mediocrity was prevalent. In contrast, the last union-negotiated employment contract for one of us was 69 pages long. It was dense with terms and conditions of employment.

The third factor cementing sameness is the rise of NPM / professional management in universities. Much of this is directed at responding to the requirements of the TEQSA, the ERA and the legislation under which each university receives its charter. Also, there now seems to be a need to manage an ever-growing number of risks within the university environment, such as OH&S, staff welfare, student welfare, student malpractice, research malpractice, cyber risk, data risk, ethical risk, operational risk, financial risk, regulatory risk, crisis risk, climate risk, reputation risk. Professional risk consultants have targeted universities to help them assess their vulnerability, design programmes to manage risk and recover from risk failures.

A rich and successful history plus these institutional mechanisms have combined to produce a higher-education sector with few meaningful differences. In commercial situations where there is an inherent sameness across members of a strategic group, such as the Big 4 Australian banks, one often observes artificial attempts to differentiate one institution from another. Corporate identity, branding and communication are often used for this purpose. The websites of the universities are revealing here. They are marketing devices. The first screen looks more like the package of a supermarket product than the front door to an organisation with a deep purpose. And from here they explode to reveal all the complexity of the institution's operations. At our last university there was a group of 28 administrators tasked with managing the institution's marketing and communications, and a further 36 responsible for brand strategy and engagement. As old marketers, we think that 64 people are not necessary to tell students about the university, especially when research suggests that many students get most of their information via WOM—word-of-mouth and word-of-mouse.

9.4 Staging

The strategic narratives of most universities suggest that they are constantly making changes to their operations to exploit opportunities and overcome obvious problems. Explore the website of any university and it is easy to find examples of new programmes being launched and new people being appointed to run such initiatives. There is no shortage of activity. For example, in the area of education each university seems to have adopted a different approach to learning. Their websites reveal learning philosophies like blended learning, block learning, flipped learning, group-based learning, case-study learning, student-led learning, work-based learning, problem-based learning, active learning, active and inquiry-based learning, flipped classrooms, design thinking, MOOCs and so forth. Long gone it seems is the era of 'chalk and talk'.

In the area of research while most activity still occurs within faculties, these endeavours have been supplemented with cooperative research centres, university and industry partnerships, and cross or multi-disciplinary research centres. The easiest way to explore new areas of interest seems to be to bolt-on a new research centre. The University of Western Australia's annual report notes it has 45 of these. From an NPM perspective these are an interesting idea because they allow the university's administrators to measure efficiency and performance. It is clear what they cost to run, what independent money they attract and what they produce. And because of their insular nature, they can be closed down if performance does not meet expectations.

Another staging mechanism is the branch office. Some are local, such as a regional university with an office in the near-by capital city, and some are located in a foreign country, such as Dubai, Hong Kong, Singapore, Thailand, Vietnam. Many overseas universities have also followed this approach. All sorts of reasons are provided for why such endeavours are a good idea. However, many are not strategically sound. For example, some years ago both of us attended a meeting where the senior administration of the university suggested that a branch office of our school be opened in Hong Kong. The idea originated with an industry advisory group—'Asia is booming, there are lots of students, why aren't you up there!' At the end of the meeting one old strategy professor (who was an ex-management consultant) summed up the idea as follows:

> As a small institution with limited financial resources let's be a late entrant into a highly competitive market where it is not clear about the regulatory requirements for accreditation; where some local universities are very good, and where recent overseas entrants like us are not making any money. And, to succeed we will have to redeploy from our current programs some of our best resources in order to establish our quality.

This comment was all it took to bring sanity back to the discussion. It was also a good example of the value of harsh academic scrutiny of the 'free advice' from people without deep knowledge of higher education and no skin in the game—the industry advisors were not willing to bankroll the venture.

On a number of occasions we have been critical of the lack of a clear line-of-sight between key aspects of strategy and the financial management of the university. While we were at the University of New South Wales, one of the vice chancellors (Fred Hilmer) made the effort to inform the senior academics about the revenues and costs of the university. At our last university this information appears in the annual business plan. Also, each university publishes a set of accounts in its annual report. Given that the annual report is a public document, we will use it to raise some important strategic issues in the next section.

9.5 The Economics of a University

Chapter 1 noted that Australia's universities are happy to argue that they are under-funded. So a key question is whether this is true? A second question is whether our universities waste some of the funds they receive? Answers to both questions help to expose the Business Model and the Profit and Loss Statement of a university.

The University of South Australia is one of the few universities to discuss some of these factors. For example, by 2025 their plan is to:

- Grow the student body to 40,000, with 25% of these learning online. UniSA Online is the core asset that will support this (ad)venture.
- Generate 15% of their revenue from research activities, 60% of which will come from industry partnerships and 40% from research grants.

Now how will they grow student numbers and change the mix of research funding? Presumably, the student body will grow via the introduction of online courses. Hopefully it will not grow by lowering entry standards. So the first challenge is to make sure that these online courses do not cannibalise the revenue from their current courses. The second challenge is to do this without reducing quality. The third challenge is that they will have to compete against the online programmes of other universities in Australia and overseas. On the research front the idea is—'By growing the scale and focus of research by building capacity in areas that have demonstrated excellence and shown potential for growth'. With a large budget this might be feasible, but do they have these funds? They don't say.

On the teaching front what puts grand plans like this at risk is price discounting. For example, there is an emerging trend for universities to offer substantial tuition fee discounts, especially to attract international students. Phil Honeywood, president of the International Education Association of Australia, said that many of these discounts were dressed up as scholarships.[2] So, there is a downward pressure on fees—revenue. Competitors are just as desperate as UniSA to grow their numbers.

On the research front UniSA is exposed by its lack of reputation. A quick look at the ERA rankings doesn't put the university in the top echelon, and as noted elsewhere, many Australian academics and their universities do not have a very good reputation for their commercial acumen. So while universities would like to generate more money from industry, many research academics simply don't care what industry wants. Getting favourable recognition from peers is far more important than getting research money from industrialists that is targeted to specific projects, and some of which the university may tax.

Because the economic logic of a university can be partly deciphered from its annual accounts, this is where we turn to next.

9.6 The Funding Game: The Revenue Model

At the 2018 *Australian Financial Review Higher Education Summit*, Anthony Walker, a director of sovereign and international finance ratings at S&P Global, said that there is a game being played by the government and the universities. Because of budget pressures, the government wants to reduce its funding of universities while they want more funding, so the truth about what is an appropriate level of funding is likely to be somewhere in between. His analysis suggests that many universities have operating margins of between 8 and 10% and quite healthy cash flows.[3] Yes, some universities might be in less than good financial health, but there is a moral hazard here—the government is highly unlikely to let one of them become insolvent. So, maybe the overall financial health of the universities is not as woeful as often claimed.

At this summit Philip Clark, a former federal government advisor on education, makes another point about the funding of the universities, namely that relying on the high numbers of overseas students, many of whom come from China, is a risky strategy. There are two financial risks here. One is that if overseas student revenue is used to 'balance the books', a downturn in demand puts the university's short-term revenue at risk. This was dramatically illustrated during the COVID-19 pandemic. The other is that if this revenue source is used to fund long-term investments in infrastructure or research, a downturn here puts these at risk. So, even though it is a luxury good in China to have an education from a Group-of-Eight university, if the Chinese government or other circumstances mean that these students stop coming to Australia, this revenue steam will stop very quickly. Also, an adverse change in the exchange rate or more restrictive student visa requirements quickly reduces the flow of international students.

Strategists like to look at what they call the revenue model of a business enterprise. In the university context, the focus is on the principal sources of revenue. To illustrate this, we will look at the 2017 Annual Report of the University of Western Australia (UWA). Here we see that UWA had $977million income for an underlying result (sustainable surplus) of $18 million. Approximately 54% of this revenue was sourced from the Federal and Western Australian State Governments. Fees and charges were $195 million (20%), other income was $100 million (10%), research income was approximately $37 million (4%) and interest was $39 million (4%).

In summary, UWA is a big enterprise that relies for about half of its income from government funding, and it generates about one-third of its income from student fees. Hence, government relations, cost control and financial management are key skills. There is nothing surprising here. However, think about research. The reputation of the university is only strong enough to generate 4% of income from this source. This is the same amount generated by the investment committee of council. What these figures suggest is that the external demand for UWA research seems to be very small.

A little further digging through the annual report reveals another interesting observation. The university had 24,327 students of whom 14,791 were fee-paying undergraduates, and 7,587 were fee-paying coursework postgraduates. These students are serviced by five faculties (one of which is very small). One of the super-faculties comprised the cheap-to-run faculties, namely, arts, business, law and education. This group educates 51% of the university's undergraduates, 37% of coursework postgraduates and 23% of research postgraduates. This pattern suggests that this faculty is <u>the</u> cash cow for the rest of the university. It is like a giant ATM from which other parts of the university withdraw their weekly allowance. As a member of this super-faculty, you could feel proud—your efforts fund much of the rest of the university, or unappreciated—your efforts are unrecognised by others. Getting the economic mix of this core funding cross-subsidy game correct can make or break the finances of a university. It can also damage the reputation of the university if in a faculty like education, student entry standards are lowered to fill up the numbers. At the time of writing, this was a topic of conversation in the media.

When compared to the great universities in the USA, the piece of the revenue model that is largely missing from Australia's universities is its endowment. While there are many reasons that might account for the paucity of Australian university endowments, the stark fact is that these institutions do not have access to a significant amount of this revenue. Much of the money given to universities comes with constraints, such as to be used for a specific piece of infrastructure or type of research. And even sponsored academic positions, such as named chairs, are rare. As government funding becomes more constrained, the need for this type of income becomes greater. Imagine the opportunities that could be pursued by an Australian university with a couple of billion dollars in its war chest!

The Cross-subsidy Game

All Australian universities have a group of low-cost faculties and degrees—the cash cows that are used to fund the high-cost degrees—the stars. The star disciplines are generally the ones that underpin the major university reputation ranking systems. They are also the disciplines that tend to make the major scientific breakthroughs that get publicity on the nightly news and in television natural science documentaries. The deans of these disciplines are generally the most powerful academic voices inside the university. At UWA these are all sciences—science, health and medical sciences, engineering and mathematical sciences. Notwithstanding the economic significance of the cash cow faculty to UWA finances, in the annual report, the exploits of the sciences are given much more prominence than law, business and education.

Cross-subsidies lie at the heart of university growth. If an institution decides to grow by increasing the size of its high-cost faculties, it will generally have to generate more revenue from its less costly faculties. This can be done by enrolling more students, raising tuition fees, reducing the delivery costs of teaching and research or clawing back more of the current revenue from these faculties. However, if the institution grows only the less costly faculties, it has free cash flow to spend as it pleases. Thus, the economic modelling of these institutions is a critical component of strategy. This is seldom mentioned outside the executive suite.

Cross-subsidies, however, come at a price to reputation and social equity. Consider the following paradox—or as Ross Gittins, economics editor of the *Sydney Morning Herald*, calls it 'short-changing their students'.[4] Step 1 is to attract students to cheap-to-provide occupational degrees—that have good job prospects like commerce, or a good image but fewer job prospects like law. Step 2 is to teach these undergraduates in large classes or substitute technology for face-to-face teaching. Step 3 is to agree to charge them a premium price.[5] Step 4 is to use the free cash flow to pay the university administrators and cross-subsidise research and teaching in other areas. Now the paradox here is that even though our universities wish to project themselves as model social citizens, an unemployed or underemployed student from a cash cow faculty soon discovers that they have been sold a degree that is not worth as much as they thought. Just like most of their business counterparts, transparency is not generally one of a university's core values. In big business, and this is what our universities are, you keep your business model out of public view.

The alternative to cross-subsidy is internal privatisation. For example, some US and European universities have allowed their business schools to retain their revenue and pay only a minimal contribution to the rest of the university. As David Kirp describes for one US school, this allowed it to raise salaries and improve facilities while salaries were frozen and faculty needs were not met in other parts of the university.[6] Any faculty with strong student demand and/or demand for its research could advocate for such a strategy. So from a strategic perspective, should a university allow any or some or all its faculties to 'privatise'? You will not find this strategic question discussed in any public statement. However, the pressure to (partially) privatise can be seen in the internal budgeting practices of the university. When universities adopt performance as opposed to activity budgets, it encourages their units to become (more) self-supporting. Chief financial officers argue that it brings more discipline to the budget process and greater internal transparency. Academics in smaller faculties might argue that it diminishes the overall contribution of the university. Vice chancellors need to make some tough strategic choices here.

The R & D Game

Public universities by their nature have adopted an open, distributed model of research transfer through publishing research and educating people who then enter the workplace. While education provides revenue, publishing gives away much of the university's new knowledge to the publishing houses, which then sell it back to them (through subscriptions to their journals). To try to get some return from their research, some universities have entered the publishing game via their university press or by publishing a journal or two or three. If successful, both revenue and reputation flow back to the university. However, in Australia the more likely outcome is a university press that publishes short production runs and seeks not to put too much drain on the parent institution's finances.

The open model of research transfer puts a considerable strain on university finances. To help counter this, the universities now ask their academics to raise more of their own research funding. Securing Australian Research Council competitive research grants is highly prized, both for revenue and for reputation. However, this and other forms of funding come at a cost. The grant writing and peer-review process are very time-consuming and highly problematic. They generate considerable amounts of stress for the people forced to seek these funds. And then when funds are secured, most academics need help navigating the university accounting, reporting and intellectual property policies.

At a National Press Club address Professor Ian Jacobs lamented about the underperforming state of business-university collaboration in Australia. His model is that the entire research pipeline moves from discovery, to translation, to application, to commercialisation. Our universities tend to focus on discovery, and industry on commercialisation. His strategy to help fill the gap was to ask government for more help in the form of things like better tax incentives for university-business projects, government co-investment in research projects and specific funding for translational research. The strategy here is to move down the value chain. Along these lines, in 2017 the British commercialisation company IP Group committed $200 million to help some the Group-of-Eight universities commercialise their research.[7]

Because this is such an important issue, it is worthwhile thinking about alternative models of research transfer and the roadblocks to such initiatives. The different initiatives respond to the different needs of organisations. Here are some further ideas.

Engaging with Industry

One was noted earlier in our description of working in the Australian Graduate School of Management. Business (and engineering) schools are closer to industry than many other faculties on a university campus. In the business school where industry collaboration was easiest to achieve, and where it seemed to have most impact, was when we were invited into a company to educate its managers. This generally involved customising our MBA course material to address a specific internal need. One crucial design element of many of these in-house courses was that the presenter would emphasise the role of evidence and research as inputs to management decisions. This was a good way to get research inside a company and to get decision-makers comfortable with using research in management practice. This is a good example of industry collaboration based on the perceived strength of the academic community (teaching). However, unlike the Harvard Business School we did not leverage this activity into writing case studies and selling them to other business schools. Our performance appraisal KPIs did not reward such 'clinical' activity. They do at Harvard.

A second approach is for the university to encourage and help its students to start their own enterprises, using what they have learned and discovered at university. This goes beyond offering courses in entrepreneurship. It requires a venture-capital approach to funding and mentoring new enterprise development. The idea here is for universities to formally invest in the new enterprises created by their students. The IP Group has also put $4.5 million into Australian university research start-ups.

A third approach is for universities to promote to their researchers the benefits of working more closely with national laboratories (like the CSIRO), and government departments and agencies (like the Australian Institute of Sport). There are hundreds of these that span many areas of interest to the academic community. They also have their own funding that will support various types of research projects. These alliances are generally perceived as 'safer' than the next option.

A fourth approach is for the universities to develop strategic partnerships with key innovative companies. Old companies like Cisco, Exxon, General Electric, Hoechst A.G., IBM, Monsanto, Rolls-Royce and Siemens have collaborated with universities for years, and new companies like Amazon, Facebook and Google also work with universities. Because many companies adopt an open innovation approach to new product development, the basic research done in universities extends the workbench of both parties.[8] The challenge is to get both parties to work together. What will often impede the development of a close working relationship is different goals, expectations and rewards of the parties and, more recently, squabbles over intellectual property rights.[9]

A fifth approach is to start a new academic hub. For example, the Australian National University has created its 3A Innovation Institute (Autonomy, Agency and Assurance) to create new applied science focused on managing the artificial intelligence and big data revolution. Many universities are 'playing' in this space with similar academic-industry collaborations. Many are also trying to entice students to join these initiatives by offering specialist (master's) degrees.

A sixth approach is to start or expand university consulting units. This type of work tends to focus more on problem solving than innovation. For example, the University of New South Wales has a professional enterprise called Unisearch that provides expert witness services. The University of South Australia has the Ehrenberg-Bass Institute for Marketing Science that collects money from companies to gather data on patterns of consumer behaviour, which are analysed to provide insights back to these companies. Other universities do sponsored research for specific industrial companies. While this is not without controversy, especially in some fields like pharmacy, in other fields like market research, there are fewer pitfalls. Where difficulties arise is when working with industry becomes transformative and some vocal staff claim that the institution's academic values may be compromised. Then contracts are required to provide confidence that conflicts can be managed, and leadership is required to endorse the principle that externally funded research is permissible and desirable.

A strategic advantage of building up industry engagement is that it often provides insight into future research opportunities. Thus, engagement becomes a dynamic capability focused on sensing research opportunities and seizing other-peoples' money to explore these issues. In the USA one of the biggest sources of funding for such future-oriented research is the military.

From a goal-setting and incentive point of view, industry engagement activities need to align with university and individual key performance indicators. Three current metrics are funding, impact and engagement. So research that is of interest to industry can secure new funding. Then to create impact, the university and its research teams need to add an advocacy element to their research. This can be done by a public relations effort to explain who needs to know about the research and what policy is necessary to implement the findings. Finally, engagement can be facilitated by the research team 'consulting' with the parties who will use the research findings. They help organisations use the findings to solve their problems. Research funding without specific advocacy and engagement often falls short of its promise.

Roadblocks

While all these initiatives could be helpful, they don't address some of the key reasons why too few academics work directly with industry and why many business enterprises are somewhat reluctant to work with academics and their universities. Here are some roadblocks that need to be addressed before a university's goal of significantly greater industry-university collaboration is likely to be met:

- We don't understand each other: Business often find it difficult to identify if a university has any knowledge of interest to them. Research academics have their own interests that may or may not have any practical implications. So the base condition for both parties is to politely ignore each other.
- Training and focus: Doing a PhD can be a brutal process that imprints a certain way and timescale for doing research. Also, the motivation for doing this piece of research is often grounded in the existing scholarly literature rather than in the field of practice. So in many disciplines PhD students follow the university mission outlined earlier by Brian Schmidt, namely, they want to add to the stock of knowledge rather than solve a problem that is troubling industry.
- Because approximately 50% of new PhD graduates now enter industry, various programmes have been designed to help these graduates migrate to a non-university workforce. For example, the APR.Intern programme focuses on getting students internships across all sectors of industry. What both employers and graduates are finding is that doctoral training provides many transferable skills that enhance workplace performance.[10] However, many of these skills often need some reshaping before they 'work' in the workplace.
- In academic performance appraisals, working with industry tends to rate behind research publications in the top-rated journals. Also, few of these journals focus on industry problems. And excellent teaching evaluations are often not related to industry engagement. So if universities really want their academics to work more with industry partners, they might consider rewriting the contracts of some chosen academics. The Harvard Business School case noted earlier has solved this problem.
- Taxing industry funding: In order to pay for overheads, there are a number of ways in which universities can 'tax' research money from outside sources. Hence, from the point of view of the patron, not all their money goes to the nominated research topic. This can detract from the perceived value of their contribution.
- Academic reputations: In Australia many academics have a reputation for being not very commercially astute. They live and work 'in an ivory

tower'. Their research is 'just academic'. They are too slow. Doing linkage research with an industry partner is too bureaucratic. And so the list goes on. So many Australian academics are handicapped by their reputation and that of their parent university. Many organisations would rather seek help from dedicated research institutions like the CSIRO or hire a freshly minted PhD who has not been too 'corrupted' by the academic environment. In many cases what makes academic research so powerful is also what makes it less than timely in a commercial setting. Good research especially big-bang breakthroughs, takes time and is plagued by missteps, things that industry can't easily accommodate.

- Track record: Over many years we have seen repeated intellectual failures across many sciences. Recent memorable examples are (a) the failure of (financial) economists to predict the global financial crisis, and once it was underway, to recommend ways to fix it, and (b) the failure of political scientists to predict the election of Donald Trump to the US White House, and that British citizens would vote to leave the European Union (Brexit). If academics can't provide clear insight into episodes such as these, why should we expect industry to rush to collaborate with universities?

So if open research transfer is laudable but expensive, and industry collaboration is somewhat problematic, there is a lot of work to be done before industry will come rushing to seek help from Australia's universities. Yes, there will be ad hoc pockets of success, but universities need to take a realistic look at their strategic and financial goals for this activity.

9.7 The Funding Game: The Cost Model

Like every large organisation universities have a diverse cost base. However, a quick look at the University of Western Australia's (UWA) annual financial statements reveals that the biggest cost is people. About 60% of total expenditure is classified as 'employee-related expenses'.

Earlier we noted that many, if not most, Australian universities have at least as many, if not more, administrative staff than academics. In 2017 the UWA staff numbers were:

- 42.9% in non-academic units
- 10.7% professional staff in academic units
- 5% professional research staff
- 16.2% research only academics
- 3.3% teaching only academics
- 21.7% teaching and research academics
- 0.2% academic other staff.

So the people in administrative roles outnumber the front-line academics (42.9–41.2%).[11] This situation is slightly more in favour of the administrators if we add some of the 10.7% of professional staff in the academic units to the administration count. These percentages reveal direct administrative costs. But it gets worse. Because nearly every academic will be involved in some form of faculty administration, then part of their salary should also be allocated to the total university administration cost. For example, in 2015 in the University of Sydney there were more than 150 faculty committees involved in administration.[12]

Another interesting picture emerges if we look at non-salary costs. For example, in 2017 the non-salary budget was just under $244 million. Then add to this—student expenses of $48 million, materials and supplies of $28 million, repairs and maintenance of $22 million, finance costs of $6 million and other expenses of $131 million and we get a total of $479 million before a single class is taught or a single research paper published.[13] This is a lot of money to run a medium-size university. Most other Australian universities look similar.

Compliance Costs

Multinational corporations and other large organisations spend millions of dollars and millions of hours of employee time each year on compliance. The belief is that rigorous compliance programmes reduce the motivation for employee wrongdoing. Also, if an employee does something wrong, the regulator and the institution's insurance provider will note that at least the organisation actively tried to avoid such a problem. The aims of these programmes are (a) to get employees to behave ethically and adhere to best practice, and (b) to eliminate the time-consuming and distracting regulatory and legal processes that accompany regulatory failure. But as is all too evident, these programmes don't always stop employee wrongdoing. An aggressive organisational culture and financial incentives will often drown out compliance training, especially when meeting stretch goals determine salary and promotion. For example, there are still periodic cases of administration (admissions scandals), academic (falsifying research) and student (cheating) misconduct.

All universities require that their staff do compliance training. For an administrator this is part of what they are paid to do. However, for a student or an academic it is not clear what compliance training crowds out of the daily agenda. For example, as most academics will acknowledge, teaching crowds out research and service. Anything to do with delivering or administering a course will take priority over other activities, even sometimes one's family. However, what comes next in the priority list depends on who asks for help. In the latter part of our academic careers, we have seen the people in central administration jump up the priority list, not by asking for help, but by demanding compliance. For example, this occurs when say a new teaching or reporting protocol is launched and everybody has to make changes to what they were doing previously.

Another example of a compliance cost was noted earlier. Recall that the University of Technology Sydney requires training for all staff on issues such as equal opportunity, mental health awareness, privacy essentials, communication and collaboration, consent (unwanted sexual behaviour), health and safety, legal affairs, preventing bullying and safety and well-being. At the time of writing, the consent training was being pushed throughout the university—for all staff and all students. It was mandatory for everybody. The online course took approximately one hour to complete and required a 100% pass on the quiz that followed the training module. Students were threatened with the withholding of their grades if they did not successfully complete the course; casual academics were offered one hours' worth of salary for their participation, and old professors were sent escalating emails (first by the HR system, then the head of school, then the dean of the business school, then the vice chancellor) when the system reported that they had not completed the course.

Leaving aside the legal and moral issues of such a request, the costs of this programme can be estimated as follows. From the university website we see that there were

- 44,887 students (which include 14,289 international students) × 1 hour = 44,887 hours of unpaid time.
- 3631 full-time equivalent staff × 1 hour = 3631 hours of paid time.

Now if we take an hourly rate of $50, we see that this exercise has cost the university more than $180,000 for staff.[14] And at, say, a notional $20 per hour for the students, it also has a cost of $897,740 for the students (minus one hour of their study time). So here is an administrative initiative with about a $1 million price tag. All this to address a social issue that the senior administrators in the university thought would signal the institution's commitment to social justice. To cover themselves, they sought legal advice before embarking on this course of action.

There is an important ethical issue here. Imagine the cost to a final-year student who can't get a job because there is an embargo on their grades because they did not complete and pass a non-curriculum course on a social issue for an organisation that they are about to leave. Second, there is no research that supports the claim that sexual harassment training actually works.[15] So here we see the university imposing a dead-weight economic cost on the institution and a dead-weight social cost on some of its members.[16]

Another largely hidden cost in our universities is due to quality assurance programmes. They are used to signal institutional quality. For example, there are a number of organisations that have developed best practice protocols for education. These organisations promote their programmes, and once a couple of institutions 'sign on', they chase other similar universities to 'catch up'. Many university faculties sign onto such programmes with little evidence that they work and without due consideration for the total compliance costs. For example, the business schools of many of Australia's universities have signed up to various accreditation programmes. The University of New South Wales business school advertises its membership of two such accrediting bodies, namely, the AACSB (Association to Advance Collegiate Schools of Business) and EQUIS (European Foundation for Management Development).[17] The school pays to join, pays to be certified and pays to be recertified every few years. Inside the business school, degree programmes need to be (re)shaped to fulfil the accrediting scheme's standards and someone is tasked with checking compliance. Then information has to be collected to report compliance each period. The costs easily accumulate into the hundreds of thousands of dollars for each such certification. However, there is little empirical evidence to suggest that these sorts of accreditation lead to more effective or efficient education, that they attract more students or that they allow the institution to charge higher course fees—especially when all competitors have signed onto the same programmes. However, what these programmes do is to lead to a lack of differentiation across the schools who sign on.

All of Australia's universities are plagued with hidden compliance costs. The key question is whether they deliver noticeably better outcomes.

IT Costs

One of the great paradoxes of modern times is that as information technology has advanced in leaps and bounds, it is much harder to find if these advances have had a general effect on increasing productivity. Within the university context, the productivity gains from new technology have been patchy. Many gains are the result of faster communication between people rather than better communication. But as the overuse of social media has demonstrated, new or upgraded information technology doesn't necessarily lead to better outcomes.

On a university-wide basis, many of the changes in technology are introduced because the suppliers of a platform have upgraded their offer. So the university 'keeps up to date' by adopting the latest version.

However, the benefits of these upgrades are seldom realistically estimated relative to the compliance costs of requiring thousands of staff, and students make changes to accommodate the new system. Hence, an upgrade usually causes some pockets of frustration and costly time in compliance, especially for the people who are not as IT proficient as their colleagues. Universities could save hundreds of thousands of dollars in cost if they had more staff and student input into what really needs to be upgraded as opposed to being 'led' by their suppliers.

9.8 The Big Question

Is the Australian taxpayer getting good value for money from its public universities? If a typical university like the University of Western Australia costs hundreds of millions of dollars annually before it produces a single key output, is this money well spent? And if not, where might cost savings be found?

These are difficult questions. And because universities know more about universities than governments or the media, the universities are best placed to provide the answers. Our analysis suggests that the problem is of two parts, namely, that the strategies of the institutions are underdeveloped and thus complexity and coordination costs accumulate. The other related cost is that the institutions become overstaffed and too bureaucratic. So one strategy for the government is to tighten up its funding and make each university find its own solution. Universities would do well to avoid this brute-force solution by seeking greater efficiency and effectiveness in their operations.

Notes

1. As noted in S. Leih and D. Teece, "Campus Leadership and the Entrepreneurial University: A Dynamic Capabilities Perspective", *Academy of Management Perspectives*, Vol. 30, No. 2 (2016), p. 194.
2. Quoted in S. Powell, "Discounts catch on as international lure", *The Australian* (5 September, 2018), p. 29.

3. E. Tadros, "Unis banking upside to defy funding cuts and lift margins', *Australian Financial Review* (30 August, 2018), p. 8.
4. R. Gittins, "We've turned our unis into aimless, money-grubbing exploiters of students", *Sydney Morning Herald* (17 September, 2017).
5. For example, while a degree in medicine costs much more than a degree in commerce (at the time of writing, this was $33,405 V $12,658), the student contribution in both degrees was the same ($10,596).
6. D. L. Kirp, *Shakespeare, Einstein, and the Bottom Line* (Cambridge and London: Harvard University Press, 2003).
7. As reported in T. Dodd, "Down payment made on $200 m start-up bet", *The Australian* (29 May, 2019), p. 26.
8. See, for example, M. Perkmann and A. Slater, "How to Create Productive Partnerships with Universities", *MIT Sloan Management Review*, Summer (2012), 79–88.
9. See for example, L. Frølund, F. Murray and M. Riedel, "Developing Successful Strategic Partnerships with Universities", *MIT Sloan Management Review*, Winter (2018), 71–79.
10. P. X. McCarthy and M. Wienk, "Advancing Australia's Knowledge Economy: Who are the Top PhD Employers?" *Australian Mathematical Sciences Institute & CSIRO*, May, 2019).
11. A note to the annual financial statements indicates that this group's salary is slightly less than that of the academics.
12. As reported in University of Sydney, *Improving Our Organizational Design*, Strategic Planning for 2016–2020, Discussion Paper No. 16 (September, 2015), (page 10).
13. Some people might want to add $54 million of asset depreciation, amortisation and impairment to this figure.
14. At this time, the pay rate for the casual staff was either $46.60 or $55.73 per hour (depending on their qualification). Because academic staff is paid more than this, the estimate here is low.
15. "While sexual harassment training is the most traditional approach to preventing sexual harassment, it has not been shown to do so." This statement is from—Consensus Study Report of the National Academies of Sciences, Engineering and Medicine, reported in P. A. Johnson, S. E. Widnell and F. F. Benya (Eds.), *Sexual Harassment of Women* (Washington, DC: The National Academies Press, 2018), p. 150.

16. Towards the end of 2018 a report to the council revealed that many students found that the course was inappropriate to their concerns and that many had yet to complete it. So teaching staff were asked to remind the students that their grades would be withheld!
17. For example, on the UNSW website you can't find what the letters AACSB actually stand for. You have to go to the association website and then search beyond the first page to find what they stand for. So how can these five letters really affect the decision-making of a new student if they are essentially meaningless?

10

What Are the Strategies of Australia's Universities? Strategy

So what is the dominant strategy of a typical Australian public university? Sooner or later most textbooks on strategy refer to the work of Michael Porter (of the Harvard Business School) about generic types of strategy.[1] Based on a company's competitive advantage (via its cost base or differentiation) and market scope (a broad or narrow focus), a company can seek to implement one of three generic strategies[2]:

- Cost leadership—lower cost than competitors and broad market coverage
- Differentiation—parity cost with competitors and appeal to a number of different segments of consumers
- Focus—low cost or unique products and services targeted to a narrow segment of consumers.

These generic strategies profile the central, integrated concept of how the university goes to market. They are useful because they reflect supply-based (cost and differentiation) and demand-based (market segments) drivers of strategy. The research about them also suggests that an organisation should not try to blend various types of strategy. Sometimes this

T. Devinney, G. Dowling, *The Strategies of Australia's Universities*,
https://doi.org/10.1007/978-981-15-3397-6_10

is called 'being stuck in the middle'. In the commercial world, studies have shown that businesses that were stuck in the middle had poorer financial performance than those that adopted a more pure form of strategy.

10.1 A Differentiation Strategy

Our judgement is that Australia's public universities are following a weak differentiation strategy—distinction without significant difference. There are similarities in their cost structures and market coverage, namely, the appeal to different segments of students. Most differentiation occurs via location, range of faculties, some star faculties (such as a medical school), a distinctive approach to learning and sometimes membership of a club (like the Rural and Technology Universities groups). All of them 'look and feel' like an Australian university.On the research front the main thing that differentiates one university from another is its position in various research ranking schemes and some notable research centres. All the universities are 'research active', but some are clearly better than others. As noted in Chap.1 by Professor Glyn Davis, they lack significant distinctiveness and they have a follow-the-leader mentality.

So with a collective weak differentiation strategy in place, are there any ways one or two might break away from the pack? The MOOC innovation noted in Chap.4, based as it is on a cost leadership strategy, might form the anchor point for a different university. So if one university could use this or a similar digital educational technology innovation to significantly reduce the cost of educating large numbers of, say, part-time students, this strategy might be feasible. The challenge here would be pricing the courses to provide enough revenue to operate the university.

Another strategy might be to pursue more focus and restructure the university around a single professional faculty like Singapore Management University or a constellation of related disciplines like the International Space University (in France). Or if this is too restrictive, restructure around a set of (complementary) professional faculties, such as business and law (two of the major power houses of Harvard University). Or restructure around liberal arts and some related faculties like Princeton

University.Its aim is to be a liberal arts university for the twenty-first century. Or restructure around biopharma and life sciences. Or humanities and social sciences (HASS).Or STEMM. Or whole-of-life health and the management of the institutions that deliver these services. Or marine or climate or environmental science. Or be a university that only has full-time students and requires them to attend all classes. The possibilities are many.

Alternatively, a university could decide that its role model was an institution like the CSIRO, or a research-focused institution with many post-graduate students like the California Institute of Technology (Caltech). The aim here would be to challenge the ANU and University of Melbourne to become Australia's best intellectual capital university. Would any Australian university be bold enough to become truly intellectually elite and seek to only employ the best-of-the-best to educate only the best-of-the-best?

In fact, any type of significant differentiation may inject a new dose of competition into the higher education sector and offer some meaningful alternatives to academics and students. The more likely scenario is that Australia's universities will continue to move in lock-step with each other. By maintaining their points-of-parity they present a somewhat united front to government to help maximise their bargaining power for support. They also present a somewhat uniform image to potential students and society as a competent group of public institutions. There would be competition, but not too much competition.

For the sake of illustration, let's assume that weak differentiation and weak competition will persist. So what might a university do? This is a marketing challenge. Interestingly, inside many of Australia's public universities is a group of people who can help their institution to develop or at least oversee this challenge. They reside in the business school. They teach and research and often consult to other organisations about marketing and strategy. However, seldom are they asked to help their own university. This lack of engagement sends an interesting signal inside and outside the university. Inside, the signal is that these paid specialists are not good enough to help. Outside, the signal is that because these paid specialists are not engaged by their own institution, why should an outside organisation listen to them. In contrast, the best professional service firms in the world listen to their own people. Could you imagine the senior management group of McKinsey & Company not listening to its own internal experts when it sets its own strategy?

So from the perspective of two strategy and marketing professors, here are some ideas.The focus is on creating some meaningful points-of-difference.

10.2 Potential Points-of-Difference

One of the primary tasks of marketers is to identify how competing brands meaningfully differentiate themselves. What makes Apple really different from Samsung? In the past it was Steve Jobs and his obsession with making the very best personal technology products. He personified Apple and linked the company to the image of Silicon Valley. In contrast, Samsung was just a Korean company that made some very good products.

So what makes one Australian university meaningfully different from another?Earlier we noted the surface differences—attributes like location, size, range of faculties, reputation ranking and so forth.But some universities have subterranean differences like their organisational culture (their core beliefs, values, rituals and people), industry engagement (tactical or strategic) and portfolio of courses (focused or diverse). Once understood, these differences might provide meaningful points-of-difference.

Organisational Culture

Over time some organisations develop a strong culture because the key stakeholders share similar and compatible basic beliefs. For example, McKinsey & Company is one of the world's best known strategy consulting firms.Its nickname is 'the firm'. And it has a strong distinctive culture anchored on client service. Some Australian readers will be aware of Macquarie Bank—nicknamed 'the millionaires factory'. It also has a strong, distinctive culture, part of which is the internal contest amongst competing ideas and projects. Strong distinctive organisational cultures attract and repel staff and customers. Only certain types of people will want to work for, and work with, these organisations.

As Fig.7.1 in Chap.7 suggests, the key groups of stakeholders in a university are academic staff and students. So what brings these two groups together to create a powerful culture within a university? We suggest that it is something as simple and as complex as why they go to, or work at, a particular university. Are they attracted to University X because theylive-to-work, or work-to-live, or because they have a calling to research or education? The features of a university that attract the 'I live because I love the work' group may not be as important to the 'I work to afford to live' group. And sometimes the behaviour of one group will antagonise another group.

Many, many years ago the old University of Chicago attracted staff and students who lived-to-work. The academic staff wanted to be surrounded with bright, full-time, hungry-to-learn students. The students wanted access to the academics, some of whom were the best in their field.Both groups liked to reside in a marketplace for ideas. Hard work was embraced. They disliked bureaucracy. And staff and students were comfortable to be judged by their outputs (such as student grades, academic publications) as well as their inputs (such as classes attended/taught, committees attended).In contrast, many of the people we have worked with over our academic careers are best described as 'work-to-livers' who are attracted to a comfortable university culture with little internal competition, clear protocols to guide their work and performance judged by inputs rather than outputs.Occasionally when we visited a US regional university, we saw people who had a calling to university life. These folks were the ones that did a good job with their teaching and research but added a degree of pastoral care to students and other staff that was above and beyond the call of duty.

While most of Australia's universities make some glib statements about their values, great staff and social inclusiveness, they tend not to emphasise a distinctive culture of the university, especially one that suggests that it has an uncompromising approach to research and education. One potential exception is the Australian National University (ANU).The ANU trumpets its place as Australia's 'national university' and its first place amongst Australian universities in many university rankings.Its strategy statement (2018–2021) also contains a section titled 'building on a culture of academic excellence'. Here it claims (without evidence) that it will lead its peers in the recruitment of the best academics and apply the highest performance standards. It will also maintain the most demanding student-entry requirements (again without evidence). And a search of the university website will uncover an internal procedure for periodically accrediting each academic school and department.

There are many staff and students who would be attracted to such a high-performance organisation. And many employers would welcome the graduates from such an institution.

Industry Engagement

Engagement with industry seems to be something that the government wants, many students would welcome and some sectors of industry encourage. So every university says it wants to do more of this.However, as we noted earlier, many of Australia's universities are struggling to design strategic responses to this opportunity. The challenge here is to pick an approach that works, and thus will meaningfully differentiate the university from its peers.

Because picking winners is difficult, what we see is that many universities adopt a venture capital or fast-failure approach to their industry engagement. They ask their academics to propose research centres that might be able to engage with industry. Successful applications are then given some seed funding by the university. A professor is tasked with leadership, fundraising and industry engagement. The university then sits back and watches and waits. Success is applauded and failure quietly closed down. As the University of Western Australia's 45 research centres illustrate, a university can spread its bets.

In contrast to these fractional approaches to industry engagement, consider the approach adopted by Macquarie University under the initial stewardship of Professor Stephen Schwartz.The university began an industry-engagement strategy which has now become a key part of the Macquarie Park Innovation District (in Sydney). The university, its hospital and its innovation incubator share this district with companies like Abbot, Cochlear, CSIRO, Fujitsu, Johnson & Johnson, NAB, Orix and

3M.The Universities of Melbourne and Queensland have also set up similar corporate arrangements.In the UK some large academic health science centres designed to speed up the 'bench to bedside' cycle of fundamental research have emerged. And some regional UK universities have identified the need to undertake some 'arrow projects' which are targeted specifically at local industries and small to medium-sized enterprises.[3]

In these types of situations a university becomes the core-in-the-cloud of industry R&D centres, think tanks and other research institutes. These institutions draw intellectual strength from the university and in return provide it with financial, human and physical resources.Because they are also more flexible and adaptive than a university, this relieves some of the pressure on universities to change as fast as the outside world seems to be.In today's world of electronic communication, these networked institutions need not be physically located next to a university.

However, as Mark Dodgson and Jonathan Staggs note, it takes foresight, time, university strategy, political help and often some significant donations to create initiatives like an industrial park (Macquarie), a health sciences cluster (in Melbourne) and the Smart State Institutes in Brisbane.[4]It also takes some academic entrepreneurs with ambitious agendas and a massive commitment to the cause. So if Australia really does want to ramp up its competitive research infrastructure, some of our universities will need to make significant strategic commitments of time and resources to a particular area of endeavour. The companies that can contribute and benefit from this infrastructure will also need to make major commitments to forming strategic partnerships with the core universities.

If clearly defined, a specific type of industry engagement, or non-engagement, could become a meaningful differentiator for a university. Or to be somewhat contrary, imagine if a university said that it did not do industry engagement, but rather it was led by its basic scientific compass. Imagine if it was bold enough to proclaim that rigour was more important than relevance. That it favoured the philosophical over the practical. That its research goal was simply to add to the stock of human knowledge. This would be a significant point-of-difference.

Course Proliferation

All universities try to accommodate the needs of different types of students by designing different types of degrees. The strategic issue is how many degrees are necessary to accommodate student diversity without causing confusion or blowing out costs? The preferred way to attack this problem by many Australian universities is to survey students and then offer degrees to meet their needs. For example, at the time of writing, the University of Technology Sydney's Business School discovered that some students wanted a standard MBA degree as a bridge from, say, arts, law or engineering into business (2 years full-time or 4 years part-time @ $62,784), while somewanted an advanced MBA (1 year full-time @ $49,365),others wanted an MBA to help them become an entrepreneur (1 year full-time @ $48,024),andstill others wanted to do their MBA with people like themselves who have at least 5 years of work experience at a managerial level (2 years part-time @ $71,800). So UTS offers an MBA, an MBA in Entrepreneurship, an Advanced MBA and an Executive MBA.And yes it seems odd that it takes less time and it is cheaper to do the Advanced MBA than the standard MBA![5]

When each faculty within a university follows the path of 'the more we offer, the better we look', you can easily wind up like the University of Newcastle (UoN).In 2017 it offered 220 degrees through 16 schools in 6 faculties to approximately 37,000 students. So it seems that UoN is trying to look big like its peers—broad scope, and different to its peers—we have some bespoke degrees. In marketing, this situation is called a product/brand proliferation problem. It occurs because old products/degrees are much harder to remove than new degrees are to install. And as new people take over an area, one way to signal their arrival is to introduce something new. The problem with university degrees is that each one has a set of administrators and administrative systems attached to it. So you don't just grow degrees, you also grow their administrative support. Sooner or later someone in authority will decide to prune the portfolio. From an economic perspective, reducing the number of degrees reduces the costs of administration and the costs of complexity.

Having identified some points-of-difference, the task shifts to communicating these to the people who matter.

10.3 Communicating Points-of-Difference

In marketing, differentiating what are essentially similar product offerings usually involves selecting a primary point-of-difference that will pass the IDU Test, namely, is this difference Important to key stakeholders, Deliverable by the university, and Unique? Passing all three criteria is hard to do.Because it is done best and sometimes worst in commercial settings, here are some examples.

Some time ago when developers were trying to build the world's tallest buildings, they were prone to advertise that their hotel (or whatever) was the tallest in the world (or in Asia or some other region). While this was often true (deliverable and unique), most people other than the developer and the owner didn't really care. It was not a point-of-difference that helped the building function better or to attract more than passing patronage.

The best companies in the world know how their strategy makes them special. This is often a strategic capabilities and/or customer value proposition approach to positioning.Consider 3M—a company that spends more money on research than probably any single Australia university.It has a strong innovation culture, a related operational capability and an envious track record of new product development. Its old corporate slogan was one word—'innovation'. Its new one is 'Science.Applied to Life.'General Electric is another research-led powerhouse. It has its own internal university. However, because it has a varied set of divisions, its corporate slogan communicates what all these entities are designed to do, namely, 'we bring good things to life' (create them and bring them to people's lives).It kept this slogan for 25 years. In 2003 it changed to 'imagination at work', which is 'same, same, but different' to many of its industrial peers. A look at the websites of both these innovation-led companies showcases their achievements.

Another notable approach to positioning is to make a promise to a target customer group and consistently deliver it. Older readers may remember when FedEx entered the US market.Its promise was overnight delivery. Its advertising said 'when it absolutely, positively has to be there—overnight'. Here the focus was on the target customer's need. The logistics capability that allowed FedEx to do this was left in the background. So along comes a major competitor DHL. It can also deliver overnight, but how can it match this promise? It focused on the emotional uncertainty that the courier might not deliver the package.Its advertising said 'as sure as taking it there—yourself'. The best and most memorable of these slogans are the ones grounded in the strategy of a company. They speak to the target customer, but more importantly, they remind every employee about why they come to work.

So how could an Australian public university think about meaningfully differentiating itself from competitors? Elsewhere when writing about creating corporate reputations, one of us suggested that companies should consider using what is called a Simply Better approach to positioning the organisation.[6] Here, the idea is to select a position that conveys excellence on some attribute that is important to stakeholders, for example:

- Best For—a particular group of people, such as postgraduates
- Best At—a particular function, such as digital technology
- Best of Breed—simply the best university in Australia
- Best Because—of a particular capability, such as marine science
- An Expert—in the field of, say, medical education for general practitioners

While these are all slight differences on the theme of excellence, as illustrated later when discussing how some German automobile manufacturers talk about themselves, a good advertising agency can help communicate a version of excellence that will resonate with stakeholders.

All these positions require assembling a set of points-of-proof.For example, the Best of Breed position is often signalled by the consistent first place ranking in the most prestigious reputation poll. The key here is that such a point-of-proof must be both meaningful and defensible. Saying that a university aspires to be ranked in the top 100 universities in the world in a poll that most people don't understand is not an indication of genuine quality. Also, saying that a university wants to be known as Australia's 'global' or 'national' or 'technology' or 'regional' university is a vague aspiration, not a firm statement of achievement or difference.

Now if one of the Simply Better reputation positions is not credible, then the university will be forced to seek a somewhat weaker position, such as being the member of a Club (such as rural universities, Technology Network universities, open universities or the Group-of-Eight research universities) or located in a prestigious city (say Melbourne or Sydney) or precinct (such as the Macquarie Park Innovation District), or of a particular type (a technology university or a religious university). The idea here is to choose an attribute that triggers some positive associations for the university. For example, today the word 'technology' is in much favour. So what do Royal Melbourne Institute of Technology and University of Technology Sydney do? They tend to refer to themselves by their alphabet name—RMIT & UTS. This simply hides the word that triggers a potentially powerful association.

To illustrate the communication challenge, here is how some of Australia's public universities introduce themselves via their motto or corporate slogan:

- ANU—Naturam primum cognoscere rerum—first to know the nature of things
- UNSW—Scientia manu et mente—knowledge by hand and mind
- UTS—Think. Change. Do.
- University of Sydney—Sidere mens eadem mutate—though the constellations are changed, the mind is the same
- RMIT—Perita manus mens exculta—a skilled hand and cultivated mind
- Central Queensland University—doctrina perpetua—forever learning
- University of Newcastle—I look ahead

Uhm!!

Because these slogans were crafted early in the history of the university, we are not sure that they really help to communicate a point of meaningful difference or to remind staff and students about the telos or the strategy of the institution. Also, when a slogan is a bit abstract, it encourages the faculties to come up with their own. For example, the UNSW Business School uses its own slogan 'Where Great Minds Do Business'. (Hubris!)We think that a good advertising agency could help many of

Australia's universities create more meaningful corporate positions. The old advertising agencies were masters of this practice.

Creativity Informed by Insight

Positioning is a creative inspiration informed by research. The research is focused on understanding what is being offered and what people are really buying. The art is creatively communicating this.For example, Charles Revson, the founder of Revlon cosmetics, once noted thatin the factory we make cosmetics but in the drugstore we sell hope. While the *National Geographic*magazine is filled with interesting stories and wonderful photographs, many readers are experiencing cheap travel. When Apple launched the iPod, they said it gave you 1000 songs in your pocket. To a school child a museum of natural history is a dead animal zoo.To many adults a museum is a library of life. Ballet is art that moves. Depending on who you are, IT means information technology, inspiration technology or in trouble. A school provides education for life (life skills for the rest of your life).

Sometimes competitors want to claim the same capability as the basis of their corporate position, such as Audi, BMW, Mercedes Benz and Porsche all wanting to anchor their position on what their countryoforigin is known for, namely, German engineering. Some years ago they did this by claiming a different aspect of German engineering excellence—Audi's corporate slogan was 'progress through technology' and later 'truth in engineering'; BMW's was 'the ultimate driving machine'; Mercedes Benz's was 'engineered like no other car'; Porsche's was 'driving in its purest form'.Now how does Volkswagen find a place to dance on this pinhead? Its slogan used to be 'das auto' (<u>the</u> car).However, after the diesel emissions cheating scandal, the company decided to drop the das auto slogan in its advertising. Their new idea was to remind people that their VWs were often associated with significant episodes of their lives. So the new slogan is 'Then, Now. Always.'This is weak because many car brands could lay claim to this.

To illustrate the power of good positioning versus blather, here is a challenge to you, the reader. Without looking back can you recall any of the seven university positions described 400 words earlier? Can you recall any of the German car slogans?What about those for FedEx and DHL?What about the Apple iPod?

From a marketing point of view we are not sure that many of Australia's universities are worldclass in the presentation of the institution. A key part of the problem here is that the strategies of the universities make it challenging to identify exactly what is being sold and what is being bought.

Notes

1. M. Porter, *Competitive Strategy* (New York: The Free Press, 1980, 1998).
2. Different scholars and consultants have their own set of (generic) strategies. These three have been chosen because they are well known and fit for purpose.
3. *Encouraging a British Invention Revolution: Sir Andrew Witty's Review of Universities and Growth* (October, 2013), available from www.gov.uk/bis.
4. M. Dodgson and J. Staggs, "Government Policy, University Strategy and the Academic Entrepreneur: The Case of Queensland's Smart State Institutes, *Cambridge Journal of Economics*, Vol. 36, No. 3 (2012), 567–585.
5. This type of mixed-up portfolio also signals that the people responsible have no idea what they are doing.
6. G. R. Dowling, *Winning the Reputation Game* (Boston: MIT Press, 2016).

11

What Are the Strategies of Australia's Universities? Organisational Structure

Many of Australia's universities are not the outcome of a grand design. They have evolved over time in response to a variety of internal and external circumstances. To help navigate the university landscape,most universities publish an organisation chart. While the names in the boxes differ, the structure of most of these is remarkably similar. The charts identify governance groups (such as the Academic Board), key individuals (with status-conferring, artefact nomenclature—deputy vice chancellor, senior deputy vice chancellor, pro vice chancellor, provost and dean; and new-world nomenclature such as president, vice president, executive manager, director, chief officer), central services units (such as finance), administrative units (such as research and innovation), functional units (the academic groups / faculties) and reporting lines. The number of governance and administrative boxes always outnumbers those for the academic units. And in the game of names the old-world names and the new-world names signal a person's role in the university. Most of these organisation charts depict a managerial bureaucracy that literally surrounds the traditional faculty model of a university. So what do these organisational charts tell us?

T. Devinney, G. Dowling, *The Strategies of Australia's Universities*,
https://doi.org/10.1007/978-981-15-3397-6_11

The first thing to note is their complexity. Organisational complexity generally produces individual complexity. A complex university generally means difficulty for staff, students and outsiders to navigate to the point where decisions get made, and to find the people who are accountable for functions and decisions. It also suggests that (a) there are many 'moving parts' in the organisation that require coordination, and (b) that some of these will superimpose their will on the academic community. For example, there is often a senior administrator whose title suggests that they are responsible for developing one of those prosaic university-wide education strategies noted earlier. Hence, the academics will be encouraged (escorted) to be up-skilled in the finer points of the chosen educational strategy, and required to design their courses to reflect its philosophy, regardless of whether or not it suits their teaching style or the content of the course or the needs of the students. Operational costs and personal transaction costs rise.

To illustrate organisational complexity, consider the situation faced by the University of Sydney in 2015 when it reviewed its structure. It noted:

> The difficulties inherent in our complex academic structures are well known. Too often we see people of goodwill who are seeking to do the best by the University forced to find ways around arcane and complex structures to arrive at the best outcome.[1]

Many people who work in Australia's universities would emphasise with this remark.

The second thing of note in a university organisation chart is the number of faculties. These profile the academic footprint of the university. They are the key operational units for the delivery of the education and research aspects of strategy. They have decision rights over the two key aspects of generating revenue and reputation, namely, teaching (such as student grades, suspension, assessment, curriculum design and the award of degrees) and research (such as the hiring of academics, research training). Faculties also have significant budget responsibility. The three key roles of the faculty dean are to manage down to the academics (a leadership function), up to the chancellery (a general management function) and out to alumni, industry and other communities (a community relations / engagement function). Arguably, it is the quality of these deans that make or break the academic reputation of a university.

The reason that faculty deans are so important is that they play the role of the general manager in other types of organisations. Henry Mintzbergsummarises the role of general managers and thus deans as follows.[2] These are the people who (should) know what is happening in operations—the generation of knowledge and its distribution, and central management—setting the strategy for the organisation. The people in operations see what is happening with complete clarity because they are closest to the action. But they do so only narrowly. The people in central management see widely because they look all around the organisation. But they don't see clearly because they are distant from operations. So the job of a faculty dean is to see the parts of the university that touch students and the users of research and then swing around and talk about these issues to the people in central management. This is a very difficult, political job.

What an organisation chart doesn't tell is the strategic role and interdependence of the various faculties within the university (as per Figs. 4.4 and 9.1). For example, which faculties are tasked with generating reputation and which are tasked with generating revenue for use by other parts of the university? For example, in the University of Sydney review it was noted that at the time Michael Spence became vicechancellor the 16 faculties of the university were 'in some respects 16 universities in competition with each other' (page 6). In essence, the university was a 'multiversity'. It competed with itself for students, for the allocation of teaching loads (and thus budgets), for research grants and donations; it duplicated courses and forced collaboration to occur through an elaborate structure of centres and institutes.

The big strategic issue for the University of Sydney and many other Australian universities is the relationship amongst faculties. In many institutions there is little or no relationship amongst faculties that could or should be vertically or horizontally linked. Thus the faculties are silos—academic units that peacefully coexist without much care or consideration for their compatriots. We suggest that a university where the integration logic of its faculties is unclear or uncertain is a suspect design.

11.1 Strategy and Structure

There is an old axiom that structure follows strategy. The strategy template (Fig. 4.2) described in Chap. 4 shows this. The logic here is that as the environment changes, organisations need to revise their strategy, and this often requires new organisational structures to implement this strategy. So if Australia's universities are as responsive to change as they say they are, institutions like the University of Sydney should be able to change their structures and organisational designs to better fit their new strategies.

Over recent years both the University of New South Wales and the University of Melbourne have attempted to reorganise themselves to respond to the demands of their updated strategy and to reduce the dead-weight costs that accompanya faculty structure burdened by a managerial bureaucracy. As noted in Chap. 8, UNSW has adopted a matrix style of organisation. This 'Strategic Matrix' asks every faculty to deliver every 'priority and theme' of the institution's goals. It also asks the 8faculties, 1college and 50 schools to work across 'the organizational structure and disciplines'. The logic here is to better enable different academic divisions to tackle some of those twenty-first-century complex, cross-disciplinary problems that they call 'grand challenges' (aka wicked problems). The strategy statement hints that internal research funding and career progression will be the tools to motivate compliance. So here is what we call a 'force-fit' situation. The structure is not naturally aligned to the new strategy. It is so rigid that it puts pressure on internal KPIs to force strategy-structure fit.

The University of Melbourne has also reorganised itself into what they call the Melbourne Operating Model. Here, there are three interdependent areas of operations—academic divisions (responsible for teaching, learning, research and engagement), university services (to offer expert advice and operational support) and the chancellery (responsible for strategy, policy, capabilities, capital and brand). This structure was built on the logic that the academic divisions are the key units of production, and the role of the other two areas is facilitation. If the faculties can show the leadership required to achieve the university's telos, and the administrators can facilitate rather than inhibit, this might work.

What is interesting and reflective of other university attempts to redesign themselves is the primary motivation for a university to reorganise itself. Here the University of Sydney study mentioned earlier is informative because it outlines the reasoning behind their attempt to reorganise. The report starts by recognising the nature of the problem, namely, to simplify their complex academic structure. The report then admits that its current structure is rigid because conversations about change will be 'infected' by power, language and nomenclature. The report goes on to concede that it is impossible to have a new structure that does not adequately recognise its six largest faculties. So the way that the university proceeded to tackle the issue was for the Provost 'to advance University-wide discussion of how we might best refine our faculty structures' (page 18).

From a strategic perspective, simply trying to reduce complexity assumes that the basic faculty structure is suitable. And that efficiency and effectiveness should improve if this can be simplified. However, if the university wants to chart a new course, such as use cross-disciplinary cooperation to tackle complex problems in some key areas, then all aspects of structure should be examined. The role of the vice chancellor and the council is to set the new strategy and then design a structure that implements it efficiently and effectively. You don't start by going to the university community and asking for suggestions because most faculties, especially the big successful ones, don't want (too much) change. In fact, the existing power of the faculties, distributed as it is throughout the university, effectively blunts the institution from doing anything truly radical. So trying to force-fit a new strategy into a powerful, entrenched organisational design is a difficult task. What might need to be done is the corporate approach—bring in the high-priced consultants to provide the rationale for change and a new blueprint. And if these consultants are any good, they will charge such a large fee that the university will struggle to explain why it did not implement their advice!

Our discussions over the years with university administrators suggest that many privately agree that there is too much administration in their institution. For example, the University of Technology Sydney has a formal programme called Unleash to reduce red tape and redundancy.

So why do Australian universities have approximately twice the administrative intensity as their UK counterparts (as noted in Chap. 1)?

11.2 The Managerial Bureaucracy

Given our pale assessment of the managerial bureaucracy in universities, why did it evolve and why does it persist? As noted in Chap. 1, it started with the new public management (NPM) movement. But it was also helped because members of the academic community in many universities decided to outsource part of their administrative load in the hope that it would free up more time for teaching and research—the two functions that drove their promotion and reputation.

A number of reasons seem plausible for its persistence. One is that it is now entrenched across most public sector organisations. It has become the dominant 'institutional design'. Another is that it 'works' for many aspects of university operations. Professional managers are generally better than academics at applying their time and systems to administration. And as universities grow and governments seek to guide and control them, there is a lot to do. Another reason is that it provides a large number of people with gainful employment, as well as power and control over a large and prestigious institution. The salaries of the vice chancellors noted in Chap. 1 are signals of how important university administration is priced to be. Finally, there is an institutional rigidity to downsizing and streamlining the administration of universities. For example, the 2018 Annual Operating Report of the University of Technology Sydney reveals that professional staff numbers keep rising each year.

Our criticisms of this style of management, especially when it is populated by people from outside the academy, are twofold. First, it too often relegates academic opinion to the role of background noise. This is a mistake because it is the academic community that is primarily responsible for creating revenue and reputation. And it is the faculties that bear the burden of change and innovation. Great universities get a balance between internal, self-generated leadership and institutional management. Here institutional strategy and organisational design are the responsibility of the senior executive. And it is a mistake to ask every university constituency what they would like the university to do or how it should be organised. But, the design and delivery of service is the responsibility of the faculties. And it is a mistake to encourage institutional administrators to decide or dictate what quality teaching or research entails. This is why the University of Melbourne's three interrelated dependent areas of operation have appeal. It seems to recognise the mutual contributions of each party.

Our second criticism echoes much the corridor talk (aka whinging) in the faculties. Many administrators do not understand the ripple effects of their decisions on an academic's time. If an academic read and complied with every administrative communication, and responded to every invitation to join working groups and attend functions, their available time for educational development and research would be severely diminished. As noted earlier, given that the typical union-negotiated workplace agreement is a paid 37.5-hour week, there is simply not enough time for too much administration. And if the communications from administrators are an integral part of implementing the university strategy, then many are being ignored.

11.3 Postscript

After commissioning its extensive review of their organisational structure in 2015, the University of Sydney settled on a 'complex organization' as it is described on their website. What is noteworthy is that the organisation chart on the website does not have enough room to list the now sixfaculties and threeschools(16 units were reduced to 9). They are referred to once on the chart as 'Faculties and University Schools' in a box that suggests they report to the Provost and deputy vice-chancellor. We wonder whether the intention was to marginalise their strategic significance.

Notes

1. *Improving Our Organizational Design,* Strategic Planning for 2016–2020, Discussion Paper No. 16 (September 2015).
2. H. Mintzberg, "Musings on Management", available at https://hbr.org/1996/07/musings-on-management.

12

A New University

To prime this discussion, consider the following. There is a university in St Petersburg, Russia, that is called a University of Finance. Denmark has an IT University. In the UK there is the London School of Economics and Political Science (commonly referred to as the LSE), the London Business School and the Royal College of Music. In Singapore there is the Singapore Management University. In France there is the International Space University. There is even an institution called the University of Coffee. [1]McDonald's has its Hamburger University. The giant company General Electric has its own Corporate University. The energy company BP has a Financial University. All these institutions tell you what they do and hence what to expect.

The power of a focused position is that many people believe that the institution is a specialist and that specialists are more knowledgeable and offer better quality than generalists. Hence, an institution with a small, focused academic footprint could be introduced into the Australian system as an alternative to its conglomerate competitors. Mid-size institutions like Caltech and small institutions like the London Business School and the LSE have established their reputations as small centres of excellence.

T. Devinney, G. Dowling, *The Strategies of Australia's Universities*,
https://doi.org/10.1007/978-981-15-3397-6_12

In this chapter we describe a hypothetical specialist university, one that is focused and has an R&D culture. Our design is for Research (the intellectual capital role of the university) to inform Development (the information dissemination and engagement roles of the university). In this model Development occurs in two forms:

- innovation—new ideas, products, services, policy, start-up enterprises and so forth,and
- people—with new knowledge and ideas, social awareness and so forth.

As we have argued earlier, because the comprehensive nature of universities produces many structural inefficiencies, a specialist university that seeks economies of scope through exploiting the synergies of related disciplines and functions would provide a sound business model. Also, a specialist university would attract a sufficient number of academic staff in its chosen disciplines to provide depth in research and teaching. It would then be up to the dean to develop a culture that promotes internal research cooperation and fosters internal competition amongst the academics to outperform their peers. The result would be inherent quality and a high-performance organisation.

The Singapore Management University is a version of this approach. It has 6schools (accountancy, business, economics, law, information systems and social sciences), approximately 10,000 undergraduate and postgraduate students and 350 staff members. It is funded by government, student fees and donations. Like Australia's universities, revenue is driven by undergraduate demand; its major cost is staff salaries, and research is a cost. Where it differs is focus—on management as opposed to everything and anything. This focus provides some, but not sufficient, economies of scope to make the institution self-funding. It relies on donations for top-up funding. It also makes a modest surplus.

This is the backstory for the university described later. Because our experience is in business and management, and because it is the decisions of managers that drive economic innovation and productivity, the new university fits in with the current national agenda of enhancing the knowledge economy. We leave it to others to design similar institutions in fields such as health, the built environment, public policy, sports science, aerospace, agriculture, and so the list goes on.

12.1 The Australian Management University

Let's start at the beginning with the name of the university. For a start-up institution, it has to clearly communicate what the institution does. A made-up name for a new enterprise will only work (gain awareness, recognition and recall) if it is accompanied by a big advertising budget. So we chose The Australian Management University. 'Australian Management University' says who, where (Australian) and what it is (a university), and the 'the' positions it as Australia's best such university. This is an old advertising ploy. Recall that when BMW says that it is 'the ultimate driving machine', the other German car-makers were forced to find some other quality position.

The next consideration is the economic viability of the university. This will be driven by the demand for management education and research, and the supply of academics who can deliver these outcomes. On the demand side of the equation there is a large market for undergraduate education, as indicated by the number of faculties of business, management and economics in Australia's universities. There is also an established market for postgraduate management education, as evidenced by the number of specialist master's and MBA degrees. A new university would seek to compete with these institutions for its share of the best-and-brightest students. The demand for academic research is strong—the number of journals and book publishers is many and varied. However, the demand from industry for management research is more problematic.

On the supply side, the number of academics that can deliver undergraduate management education exceeds those who can deliver postgraduate courses. It is much more difficult to teach full-time, high-fee-paying, very motivated master's students than it is to educate more passive undergraduates. The curriculums are different, and the skills to teach intensive (often residential) courses are different to those required for large undergraduate classes. There are relatively few people who can engage work-experienced graduates with educational material that is grounded in the scholarly literature and that is relevant to current industry practice. There is a world-wide market for those who can. Through their consulting, lecturing in executive programmes and publications in magazines like the*Harvard Business Review*, some of these people establish their own brand identity. This has considerable value in the corporate guru speaker market. The best graduate school academics are often some of the highest paid in their university, and some will then double this salary with outside work.[2] In contrast, there is not a similar international labour market for people who can teach large undergraduate classes.

Given that both sides of the market are well established, both nationally and internationally, this suggests that if a coherent strategy can be developed, a primary underwriter for the new university might be interested. The federal government and a state government would be the first groups approached. Such a situation was successful in 1977 with the establishment of the Australian Graduate School of Management (AGSM). This graduate school was established by the federal government as a stand-alone unit in the University of New South Wales. In 1989 the Melbourne Business School (MBS) became its principal competitor. MBS was controlled by a non-profit company limited by guarantee and managed by a board of directors. Today it is co-owned by the University of Melbourne (45%) and various Australian businesses (55%). Until it was folded back into its parent university in 2006 the AGSM flourished as a small largely independent institution. MBS continues to flourish.

Given this background, what would the new Australian Management University look like in the current Australian context? Following the key elements of strategy introduced in Chaps. 4 and 5, let's see.

12.2 Governance

Because this is a strategy 'thought experiment', we assume that a new university could access the same sources of funds as the existing publicly-funded institutions. And like the Melbourne Business School, it might also be established as a non-profit company limited by guarantee.

In Chap. 3, we noted a number of shortcomings of the councils of Australia's public universities. In essence, most of these governing bodies do not have widespread expertise in strategy, and members devote only very limited time to their duties. Also, many of their members have a mandate of constituency representation that may clash with their responsibility to put the interests of the university first. To overcome these limitations, we suggest that governance needs some reform.

The chancellor should be almost a full-time appointment. This person should signal the character of the university, in this case a business-oriented R&D university. So a successful, well academically credentialed, senior business person would be suitable.

Other members of the council would be chosen from the university community and industry, based on their experience and expertise. University appointees would be the internal leaders of the institution. Industry appointees would have expertise in the fields of strategy, finance, risk and management. The council would look more like a board of directors than a traditional university council. The external appointees would be well paid for their work and be expected to take the time to understand the university. They would also be expected to help build strategic relationships with industry partners. The idea that a council member reads the council papers and turns up to as many meetings as possible is a recipe for ruin.

Choosing a vicechancellor is a difficult task because this person needs experience inside a university as well as in business. To have moral authority amongst the academics, the vicechancellor needs to be an ex-academic. There is nothing like surviving the pressure of teaching and having one's research peer reviewed for developing an understanding of what makes a university 'work'. To have moral authority in industry, the vicechancellor needs to have worked in some form of industry. Because professional service firms are most like universities in the sense that they are intellectual capital organisations, these could provide suitable candidates. Given that vicechancellors routinely expect a $1million salary, there should be no shortage of candidates. There is an ample supply of professional university administrators available to help such a person run the university.

12.3 Mission, Vision andValues

In the style of an R&D university in the new knowledge economy the institution would be informed by industry, guided by research and designed for (aspiring) managers, business professionals, consultants and the management academics who will inform industrial organisations.

Informed by Industry

Informed by industry does not mean that industrialists and senior members of the business professions would dictate curriculum or the research agenda of the university. What it means is that the university would need to understand and be sensitive to the concerns of various industrial groups. This would be achieved by commissioning a group of industrialists and professionals to act as an advisory board to critique ideas put forward by the academy. For example, many years ago such a group was asked if the Australian Graduate School of Management (AGSM) should follow the trend of some of its competitors to shorten the duration of its full-time MBA programme from two years to eighteenmonths. This was an idea put forward by students. The answer was a resounding 'no'. The advisory board and a survey of employers thought two years was the minimum time it took for an engineer or accountant or a lawyer or a medical practitioner to learn about business and acclimatise to become a manager of people.

For research being industry informed means 'testing' one's ideas against the opinions of people in industry and the professions before committing to a project. The best way of doing this is to seek funding from industry. If this can't be gained, the signal is that interest is lacking. While the research programme might proceed and be funded internally or by another external funding body, useful feedback has been received.

Guided by Research

As noted earlier, university-style research is a competitive advantage. It is something that most organisations in industry and the professions think that they can't afford to do. So the new university will use this type of slow, deliberate research to inform everything that it does. The example earlier about requiring every employee and student to undergo sexual harassment training is a good example of instigating a programme that was uninformed by research. It looked good to the public and the policy-makers, but the prevailing research suggests that it will be ineffective. And a few quick financial calculations revealed that it was expensive to implement.

Guided by research also means that the academic community will be consulted about major decisions. Academics often have information from their broader scientific inquires and their private networks that speaks to many issues about the strategy of organisations. Recall the case where an advisory group advised the university to open a branch office in Hong Kong. The senior professor whose summary of this idea derailed the adventure was informed by his network that all the overseas universities that had entered this market were struggling. Listening to the academic community is also a good way to foster a culture of internal leadership and accountability.

Stakeholders

The primary external stakeholders of the new university are graduates, industrial and not-for-profit organisations, their advisors and the people who are employed as consultants and managers in these organisations. Each group is expected to have some skin in the game. For example, students pay with their fees and the time and effort devoted to their education. In contrast, many companies and professional institutes are more like spectators than stakeholders. Occasionally, they offer some 'free' advice, and a few individuals offer their time. So to rectify this situation, the major beneficiary groups would be expected to fund student scholarships and endowed professorships in their area of interest.

The primary internal stakeholders are the academics who commit to the institution. As the old AGSM discovered, not everybody is suited to such a specialist organisation. Actually having to work with one's colleagues in the classroom and on business-focused research projects develops a level of teamwork and transparency about competency that soon identifies the strong and the weak. When someone's behaviour lets down his or her colleagues, the reaction from the people affected can be swift and unpleasant.

Values

The values that underpin a specialist R&D-style university can be less audacious than those grand ideas promulgated by Australia's public universities. There should be a clear line-of-sight between the institution's values and the value proposition offered to stakeholders. Three sets of values focusing on organisational citizenship, organisational culture and scientific scepticism will be important.

Organisational citizenship implies the willingness for staff to exploit synergies across various facets of business and management. The problems that business faces and managers must deal with are cross-disciplinary in nature, so academics have to be comfortable working across disciplines. Another aspect of organisational citizenship is teamwork. The way to signal this value is for the academics to co-teach classes, for their offices to be intermingled across discipline groups, for joint research to be explicitly recognised and to have some KPIs that are group based. Another citizenship value is pastoral care, namely, the development of colleagues and students. Not only is this good sense, it is something that its recipients appreciate and remember. A form of this is practised by the management consultants McKinsey & Company. Even when an employee leaves the firm (is not promoted), it keeps in contact and helps the person succeed in their career. A careers office for students and an alumni office for graduates will be complementary assets for the university.

The second set of values relate to organisational culture. Here the focus is on excellence, something the government demands, and many students and industry participants crave. A value that drives excellence is merit—of staff and students. The best graduate business schools around the world and specialist universities like Caltech and the LSE strive to capture the best students and academics. They then ensure that the process of education enhances this potential. Good staff and students plus good education should lead to good outputs, namely, in-demand graduates. For academics, merit means establishing a set of clear guidelines and KPIs that govern the hiring, promotion, firing, workload and remuneration of the academics. Meritocracy can work if it is transparent. Everybody must be able to see how standards are applied fairly across people and situations.

The next culture value is academic freedom. By this we mean that an academic can research and say what they want as long as this is informed by evidence or sanctioned by one's peers and does not damage the reputation of the institution. The way to enforce this value is to instigate what one of us has called a Reputation Rule.[3] Do something that your peers consider significantly damages the reputation of the institution and you are sanctioned. Do something that significantly enhances the reputation of the institution and you are applauded and rewarded.

The third set of values relate to scientific discovery and scepticism. The truly great universities attract scholars who discover new things and who are prepared to challenge the current orthodoxy. In the management arena, discovery research abounds and is favoured by the major academic journals. The big weakness here is that most discoveries are never replicated.[4] More emphasis here would also result in stronger foundations for the education of managers.

Scientific scepticism is another value that needs to be encouraged in a management university because myths abound and are left unchallenged for too long. Many of these originate from management consultants whose research directly competes with university research for the attention of practising managers. So a great management university should encourage some of its (older) academics to be devil's advocates—people who check and challenge management myth and ungrounded guru folk wisdom.

What is deliberately missing from this discussion of values is anything to do with social justice. Why, because after taking a long, hard look at some of these issues, we could find no evidence that imposing such qualities into an organisation has the effects on its culture or performance claimed by its advocates.[5] Yes, this type of organisational culture engineering is widespread, but it seems to be at the whim of the organisation's senior executive. While it is believed to be the right thing to do, and often applauded in the public domain, the evidence for it having a positive outcome on anything other than the superficial image of the organisation is very flimsy. So to follow the trail of the research and the principle of evidence-based decision-making, this value is ignored.

This lack of the explicit recognition of social justice principles in the institution's statement of values does not mean that unethical practices are encouraged or will be tolerated. What it does mean is that the institutional culture and the individual will take responsibility for what is deemed to be acceptable. This stands in contrast to signing up to voluntary, unenforceable codes of conduct or implementing a box-ticking compliance regime. If the individual or the institution gets it wrong, they will and should be hounded out of business. Here, having your career at risk is a more powerful moral compass than completing a course designed by some unknown group that reflects their notion of what is and what is not ethical practice.

12.4 Objectives

The previous section deliberately does not advance a grand vision for the new university. Many such university visions are simply pompous proclamations. And because they are essentially unachievable, they set the tone for the senior people not to be held accountable for failing to achieve such aims. Our preference is to set sensible, modest objectives, especially for a new entrant. So unlike the other Australian universities that all have laundry lists of objectives, here there is only one. It is found on the ground rather than in the clouds. Achieve it, and financial success then only requires some sensible cost management.

We like one of the University of New South Wales' objectives, namely, to produce in-demand graduates. Some playful expansion of this objective suggests that the university will be successful if it is in demand as a place to study by students, in demand as a place to work by academics, in demand as a source of recruitment by employers and its research is in demand by academic journals and industry. Each objective is easy to measure by the simple metric of being the first choice of students, staff, employers, journals and organisations.

Because being in demand also speaks to many aspects of university life, there will be a variety of other measures available. For example, a staff member's course is in demand if the students (over) enrol in it. A piece of research is in demand if it is published and attracts the citations of other researchers. A person is in demand if their advice and help are sought by others, if they receive offers of employment from other universities and if their ideas are listened to and acted on. The recruitment office is in demand if the students use it in preference to other avenues for gaining employment. The alumni office is in demand if graduates use it to stay connected. And so the list goes on.

Based on the simple assumption that staff, students, employers and other organisations take the time to become reasonably informed about what they are buying (into), then being in demand presupposes educational and research excellence and relevance. This assumption is based on research in consumer behaviour that suggests that when intelligent people are presented with a complex, risky buying decision, they seek information about the product and its provider to reduce uncertainty. In this case they will search across a range of different types of information to become better informed. Hence, before the new university has an established reputation, it will need some clever marketing to cater to this need.[6]

A university that is in demand because of its culture and quality does not need to slavishly play the accreditation or reputation ranking games. Needing accreditation from a commercial agency is really a sign of weakness. It communicates that the natural internal standards of the institution are weak and the university needs the help of an outside organisation to give it a Good Housekeeping seal of approval. Setting a target ranking in a reputation poll also means that the university is willing to define quality in terms of the criteria that drive these rankings rather than the criteria that create in-demand students, staff, employers and outside organisations. A good-quality, confident university defines what quality means, and its reputation naturally follows its success. It doesn't follow the lead of a news organisation that is in the business of discussing institutions to create news and sell its papers.[7]

Being indemand also comes with a massive commercial advantage—it attracts revenue, which for a start-up university will be crucial to its survival. It might also support a price premium, which is an index of quality.

12.5 Arenas, Vehicles, Differentiation andStaging

The new university is an Australian management university, so its vehicles will be education and research, and its arenas will be to conduct undergraduate, postgraduate and executive education in Australia, and research on business and management. The principal differentiator is its focus only on business and management. These activities will be staged using a blend of campus and Internet-based methods of education and research. So the new university will be a somewhat traditional institution, but one that will freely follow the best practice innovations of its peers. It will be a fast-follower rather than a disruptive innovator. Here is a bit more detail.

The Pedagogic Model

One cohort of students will be selected on their intellectual excellence. These will be admitted into traditional degree programmes. A second cohort of students will be admitted on the basis of their potential to succeed. This is an open-access approach to reflect the fact that many people's circumstance may have precluded them from pursuing a traditional path to higher education. These students will be required to complete a set of pre-degree, Internet-based subjects to a specific level of proficiency in order to be admitted to a traditional degree.

A blended learning model will be employed. It will involve the students preparing for class by accessing digital content—'read the text book before coming to class'. Class attendance will be of the tutorial style (small group, moderated face-to-face discussion) rather than 'chalk and talk'. Class attendance is mandatory. No 'lectures' will be posted on the website.

As many industry-funded student scholarships as possible will be sought to help pay for fees and living expenses. Also, industry internships will be encouraged to students and industry partners.

There is an education case and a business case for this approach. The education case is that knowledge acquisition is best done in a self-paced private environment, while learning is best done in a moderated face-to-face environment. The business case is that the expensive resource of academic time is best used in the design of the curriculum, while adjunct teachers (who might also be working in industry) can be used to guide learning. Also, the curriculum set-up costs can be amortised over as many tutorials as demand necessitates. Another advantage is that teaching spaces will be smaller and more flexible than large lecture theatres. Some of these could be rented in city and business park locations.

The Research Model

The engine room of much university research is its PhD programme. So this will be a crucial part of the research strategy of the university. However, unlike many similar programmes in Australia's universities, the students studying in different disciplines will be trained together, located together and encouraged to work together.

The inspiration of much current management research is the state of scholarship (such as filling in knowledge gaps, extending current streams of research and discovering new phenomena) and the problems faced by industry (such as how to improve performance). So the task will be to get research focused in both areas. Individual KPIs will help to get the best mix.

Because research is costly, there is a business imperative to get more of it to pay for itself. The traditional approach has been to ask researchers to seek their own funding. Australian Research Council (ARC) funding is particularly praised because it is hard to get, and because its quantum is used to signal the success of one university against its peers. However, gaining such competitive research funding is time-consuming and erratic. Also, much research needs time more than money.

For a management university, a more efficient approach would be to seek support directly from industry associations or particular organisations. An institutional approach would be more effective than asking individuals to make their own contacts. Also, sometimes the academics might need to prove their credentials before they can legitimately ask for research money. So encouraging industry-consulting assignments would be appropriate. The difficulty with this approach is to make sure that industry research 'pays off' for the researchers. So this form of engagement must result in either quality research papers or extra income that is recognised in the individual's KPIs.

The Academic Model

Good academics are a critical part of a good university, so attracting and retaining such people is crucial. The university needs a people strategy. A crucial consideration is what mix of academics is needed to deliver the quality of education and research suggested by the pedagogic and research models. Traditionally universities use a pyramid model where they employ many more junior than senior academics. The very good universities are like good professional services firms where the policy is up or out.

The pedagogic model described above suggests that a better model here is to recruit a small number of very good teachers to act as curriculum designers and course leaders. These people would be helped by technology educators to design the knowledge part of the curriculum. A casual workforce of tutors, teaching assistants and doctoral students would be used to help deliver the face-to-face part of the course. Thus, the education professorship would be a small group of permanent staff. These people would also lead the teaching of executive short courses.

The research model needs a different type of academic, someone who is comfortable talking to business and able to publish in the top journals. Only a small number of these people are needed in key discipline areas to create a research profile in the international market. This research professorship would also be responsible for the doctoral programme and the recruitment of promising junior scholars.

The final group of academics would be the Gypsy academics referred to earlier. These are identified through the networks of the academics. They would be engaged when needed as super-star teachers and researchers to enhance the offerings of the university. Their presence, especially early in the life of the new university, adds respectability to the institution. As the old Australian Graduate School of Management discovered, when these people were paid well and treated well, many academic Gypsies welcomed some time in Australia.

A key to an academic's engagement and retention is their contract. One design principle is to reward people well for what they do well, and not to pay people to do what they can't do, or don't want to do. This supports the idea that the work mix of a person should be based on their strengths. Another principle is to make sure the contract reflects the market value of the individual. Otherwise people will feel undervalued.

Together these principles mean that academics need individual contracts, not something designed by a workforce union to blanket the institution.

Another key issue is, how much is an academic worth? When we were employed by the AGSM, we were often paid less than the graduating sign-on salary of our MBA students. This type of situation demotivates many academics and is not a signal of academic quality to the students. One remedy is to pay a good salary, much above what is currently paid in the Australian university system. The downside here is that it is expensive for the institution. Another strategy is to pay what the person can bargain for. However, basing remuneration on one's negotiation skill is not a great foundation for a good citizenship culture. Another approach is to pay the going university rate and encourage people to supplement their income with up to one day per week of paid outside work. The people who elect to do outside work trade off gaining extra income against possibly missing their university KPIs which are set to disregard this time spent consulting. If people really are as good as they think they might be, their daily consulting rate and the amount of work they are offered soon (dis) prove this. Also, it takes the pressure of the institution to pay for market value. And as the Harvard Business School discovered, many academics regard their consulting prowess as an internal and external signal of (their) quality.

Target Students

For a new university the temptation is to take any students that apply. However, this tactic sets the tone for subsequent intakes. And it is difficult to raise standards over time because people tend to remember last years' entry standards. When it started on the Gold Coast, this was the problem that bedevilled Bond University. So here the tactic is to set sensible entry standards, hold them and expect small initial enrolments. The mix of students is discussed later.

12.6 Strategy and the Business Model

The size of the management education market is large in Australia, especially in its two main capital cities. If the new university was located in Sydney, it would compete directly with the University of New South Wales, the University of Sydney, the University of Technology Sydney, the Australian Catholic University and Macquarie University. As a late entrant into a somewhat congested market, the new university would need a significant cost advantage and/or a relevant point-of-difference to become established.

As noted earlier, management education and research are cheap to produce and provide relative to many of the natural sciences. Management education and research don't need high-technology, specialist buildings. As the pedagogic, research and academic models described earlier, they don't need large numbers of fixed-cost academic staff. Also, the university doesn't need to generate free cash flow to cross-subsidise other faculties. So its financial needs are modest in comparison to its comprehensive competitors. Thus the new university starts out with a comparative advantage over the existing comprehensive universities.

Given a large market, a specialist nature and a cost advantage over its local rivals, one potential strategy is cost leadership. Lower course fees would signal this strategic position. However, this low-cost position without a point-of-difference is likely to signal that the new university is a 'bottom feeder'. To avoid this perception, the initial entry position would be similar course fees with the added benefit of a more pastoral student experience. In crude terms, the student value proposition is 'more bang for your buck'. This value proposition appeals to students who seek value for money as opposed to a convenient education or one from a well-known university. This business model applies more of the fees paid by students to their education, relative to that provided by the current group of public, comprehensive universities. This would be one of the promotional themes. Another would be direct industry engagement.

The place to start would be at the top of the food chain, with an initial cohort of postgraduates plus some doctoral students. The idea here is to start out as a small graduate business school and bed down the operations necessary to run an elite institution before growing by introducing an undergraduate programme. Also, it is much easier to add a credible undergraduate programme to a good graduate programme, than the other way around. Over time, the role of the doctoral programme and academic research is to generate scientific reputation; postgraduates generate revenue and industry-relevant reputation;and the undergraduate programme generates revenue and educational reputation.

The initial marketing challenge is to communicate the points-of-difference and get a sufficient number of students to try this educational experience to generate positive word-of-mouth recommendations. As the success of 'better value' retailers like Aldi and Amazon have demonstrated, this is not an unduly difficult proposition to sell, especially when the initial number of customers needed to get started is small.

12.7 Operational Structure

Figure 12.1 illustrates how the new university would be structured. Following the lead of the University of Melbourne, there are four interdependent organisational elements—the academy, internal services, the chancellery and AMU Ltd (a professional service firm). The size of the

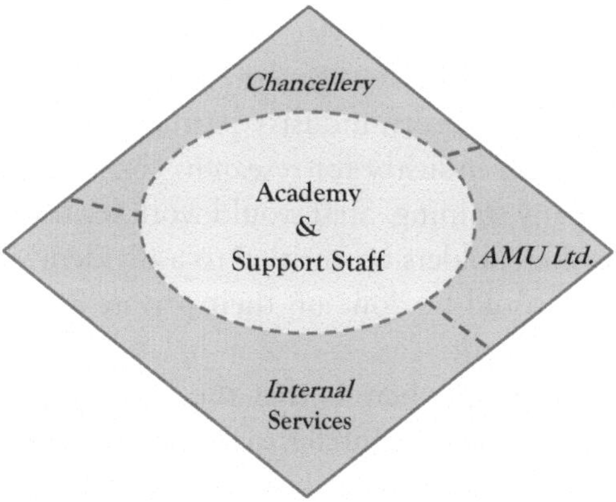

Fig. 12.1 Operational structure

elements represents their relative size (number of employees). Because the new university is specialist in nature, it does not require many of the functions found in large universities that are designed to homogenise different faculties into a single identity. Also, there are no special interest group divisions or research institutes. The university is organised more like a large management faculty rather than a down-sized comprehensive university.

The academy is responsible for education, research and academics. Education would be organised around undergraduate, postgraduate and executive programmes, each of which would be run by a small professional management team. An academic board would be responsible for establishing and maintaining academic standards. Research would be administered by a senior professor responsible for scholarly leadership. One role would be to help researchers seek funding from industry. The academic cohort would be run by a senior academic and a small management team that would be responsible for recruitment, retention and performance evaluation.

Internal services is responsible for the operational needs of staff and students (such as HR, IT, OH&S and property). The chancellery headed by a vice chancellor and supported by a small group would be responsible for strategy, engagement, fund raising, capital allocation, capability development, government liaison and reputation (and the thing that most irritates many staff and students—parking).

AMU Ltd. is a professional service firm created to commercialise the university's industrial liaison. It is governed by a board of directors and jointly owned by the university, industry partners and university staff. Its role is to contract with industry for research, consulting, expert witness work and in-company training. Staff would work for the firm, be paid for this work and as shareholders be entitled to a dividend if circumstances permit. This work would be done on their private account and thus be part of their external work.

The organising principle here is that the academy is responsible for creating and disseminating the intellectual capital of the university. They will suggest what help they need rather than be directed by others about what they should be doing. The role of everybody else is to help the efficient and effective delivery of these two roles. The principle here is that institutional complexity should not increase individual complexity.

In this scheme the vicechancellor is more of a servant of the institution and a symbolic leader than a bold path-breaking CEO. This requires consultative leadership much like the managing partner of a major professional service firm. The responsibility of the senior academics (partners) is to provide leadership from within. This type of university will succeed or fail on its quality more than the clever adaptation to current political circumstance. For the academics this is a much tougher but potentially more rewarding environment than many are currently experiencing.

12.8 Is This New University Possible?

The new management university would need

- initial seed funding, a location and a government mandate or at least its official blessing. This would establish its legitimacy. This happened when the old Australian Graduate School of Management was formed.
- to demonstrate its value proposition to attract an initial cohort of students, academic staff and potential investors, namely, key commercial enterprises.
- to rent the reputations of some key stakeholders, such as, its council members, foundation academic staff, foundation industry donors and possibly an overseas partner university.
- to seek endorsements from key business people and politicians.
- to achieve scale by successfully delivering its promise to all its stakeholders.

How Would the Incumbents Respond?

One of the reasons why this new university should be competitive is that the current universities are largely locked into their comprehensive strategy. There are two reasons for this. One is that most of the vice chancellors will be reluctant to jettison a major faculty or to amalgamate one of these with another university. The other is that strategy depends on the historic position of the organisation. Despite what the prophets of disruptive innovation suggest, few organisations can walk away from their historic antecedents, nor should they. History is more than a sunk cost. It involves commitment of resources and servicing agreements with customers that can't be jettisoned on a whim. It also defines the reputation and the culture of the institution. Only new entrants to a market can take solace in the luxury of having no past to constrain their future.

Notes

1. The initiative started in Italy in 1999 as a forum for a range of coffee professionals from baristas to growers looking to improve their business. It now does a lot of research and trains thousands of farmers a year in 20 countries.
2. In many of the major business schools around the world an academic contract typically allows the person to work up to one day per week on their private account—if their academic performance is deemed satisfactory in their annual performance appraisal. This flexibility allows the business school to attract the very best people who can earn an industry competitive salary while the school only has to pay a portion of this. For example, in the early part of this century a very good Australian business school academic could routinely charge $6000 to $10,000 per day. In 2014 Michael Porter of the Harvard Business School charged US$150,000 for a single speaking engagement.
3. G. R. Dowling, *Winning the Reputation Game* (Boston, MA: MIT Press, 2016).
4. A major reason for this is that the major journals are reluctant to publish much of this type of research.
5. For example, see G. R. Dowling, "The Glass Ceiling: Fact or Misguided Metaphor? " *Annals of Social Responsibility*, Vol. 3, No. 1 (2017), 1–21.
6. For example, it might get some celebrity endorsements from well-known academics and business people. It might get its key academics onto the publicity trail.
7. T. Devinney, G. R. Dowling and N. Perm-Ajchariyawong, "The Financial Times Business Schools Ranking: What Quality is this Signal of Quality", *European Management Review*, Vol. 5 (2005), 195–208.

13

Final Thoughts

From a government perspective, Australia needs its universities to offer a range of education services that cater to the needs of society and the developing knowledge economy. It also needs them to conduct research that informs education and the country's social and industrial development. The aspiration is that all these activities will be worldclass in nature and some will be path-breaking. The government is prepared to fund this initiative to a significant extent. However, given that the higher-education budget competes for funds with the budgets for health, welfare, defence, and one hundred other worthy uses of taxpayer funds, funding is not unlimited and some amount of self-funding is appropriate.

Australia's public universities could be much better if the relevant government ministers thought strategically about the higher-education sector. When each of the universities tries to be more or less 'comprehensive' across the sector by conducting research and education across a number of unrelated fields, there is much duplication and many pockets of mediocrity. So from a government perspective, it would make sense to look for opportunities to reorganise and consolidate university offerings and more back-of-house service functions.[1] Either the government or the universities could do this. Because government ministers come and go and are

T. Devinney, G. Dowling, *The Strategies of Australia's Universities*,
https://doi.org/10.1007/978-981-15-3397-6_13

generally under-informed about their portfolio, a better outcome is more likely if the universities lead from the front. Two simple reasons are that they know where the opportunities lie, and they have their skin in the game.

Our observation is that universities are seldom held to close scrutiny by their key stakeholders. Yes, there are government agencies that seek quality assurance and outside organizations that provide superficial rankings, but if universities had professional investors like public companies, their reporting standards would be more rigorous and scrutiny of their strategies would surely challenge many aspects of their current operations. From this perspective,we also believe that many university councils have not done an adequate job questioning and reviewing the strategies of their universities. As the title of this book suggests, we grade them as a revise and resubmit. Yes, some are better than others, but all are deficient in some major respects.

From the perspective of the current portfolio of universities, the challenge for each is to create a coherent strategy and then reorganise the institution to implement this strategy. At present the tendency is to communicate a set of lofty aims to stakeholders, with some general programmes for how these goals might be attained. These are fragments of strategy. We suggest that a strategy with more focus will result in a university that is less complex, and thus need less bureaucracy, which, in turn, will free up more resources to develop quality for whatever telos is chosen. Currently, most of Australia's public universities are over-managed and under-led.

One Last Word

Our central criticism of the current system is that Australia's public universities are too complex, so a thought from the late Steve Jobs (CEO of Apple) is timely.[2]

> People think focus means saying yes to the thing you've got to focus on. But that's not what it means at all. It means saying no to the hundred other good ideas that there are. You have to pick carefully. I'm actually as proud of the things we haven't done as the things I have done. Innovation is saying no to 1,000 things.

Notes

1. An example of a back-of-house function is the staff sector-wide superannuation schemes.
2. Reported in T. Ferriss, *Tribe of Mentors* (London: Vermilion, 2017), p. 18.

Why We Wrote This Book

The point of this short biography is to note that we have no conflict of interest in the opinions expressed in this monograph.

Timothy Devinney is an Australian-American management scholar. He currently is Professor of Management at the Alliance Manchester Business School at the University of Manchester. He previously served as Pro Dean of Research and held a University Leadership Chair at the University of Leeds. He has also been a professor at the Australian Graduate School of Management in the University of New South Wales. He is a prior co-editor of the Academy of Management Perspectives. He is a Fellow of the Academy of International Business, the Academy of Social Sciences, The Royal Academy of Arts. He was a Forschungspries awardee and Fellow of the Alexander von Humboldt Stifung.

Grahame Dowling started his university career as a tutor at the University of Newcastle (Australia) and finished as a professor at the University of New South Wales. Most of his career was spent in the Australian Graduate School of Management, where he was a member of the University Academic Board and the last Associate Dean for Research at the AGSM. In 2009 he became an Emeritus Professor. On retirement he took a part-time appointment at the University of Technology Sydney so he could walk from home to finish up some research projects. At the

T. Devinney, G. Dowling, *The Strategies of Australia's Universities*,
https://doi.org/10.1007/978-981-15-3397-6

end of 2018 he retired from UTS. At the time of writing this book (2019) he is still publishing and enjoying the role of Grey Nomad.

As marketing and strategy teachers, researchers and sometimes consultants, we were never asked to help craft the strategy of our universities. When we did poke our noses into this process, we were generally listened to with polite indifference. So why exclude the advice of the people tasked with teaching strategy to the next generation of managers? Either we can't be trusted, or we are perceived to be incompetent, or we have a reputation for being too academic or difficult to work with. (There is some truth in the last character trait!) However, if either of the first two reasons prevailed, we should have been dismissed, but we were not!

A limitation of our analysis is that it is based primarily on what are essentially institutional credential statements and public reporting documents. These are generally crafted to present the institution as a glowing example of high standards, great quality and excellent probity. However, even from this perspective, they are poorly crafted marketing documents. They are so full of hubris and puffery that at times they are embarrassing.

Another limitation is that there is information that we could not access to help underpin our arguments. Much of this relates to the internal budgets of our universities and the decision-making process in the chancellery and council chambers that commits money to strategic initiatives. If this information challenges some of our assumptions and conclusions, so be it. If it is released, we will be happy to change our position.

One of our great frustrations as old academics is the silence of our colleagues. They often moan in private about university decisions but seldom speak up in university forums. An Australian university is still one place where you can ask pointed well-informed questions to the senior managers and not be punished. So if you are a member of a university and have taken the time to read this book, please ask your university executives to explain the logic behind the strategic decisions they make. Polite questioning will get a conversation started about 'why we are doing what we are doing'. Most staff who attend the talking tours of their vice chancellor never say a word. Opportunity lost!

As with all our joint work, our names appear in alphabetical order.

Index[1]

A

[1] Note: Page numbers followed by 'n' refer to notes.

T. Devinney, G. Dowling, *The Strategies of Australia's Universities*,
https://doi.org/10.1007/978-981-15-3397-6

The manufacturer's authorised representative in the EU is Springer Nature Customer Service Centre GmbH, Europaplatz 3, 69115 Heidelberg, Germany. If you have any concerns regarding our products, please contact ProductSafety@springernature.com

Printed and bound by CPI Group (UK) Ltd, Croydon, CR0 4YY
25/09/2026
02222902-0003